Péter Mujzer

HUNGARIAN ARMORED FORCES
in World War II

KAGERO

Special thank

to Pálinkás Zsolt for his overall support to the book,
to Deák Tamás for the coloured photos, profiles.
to Bonhardt Attila, Éder Miklós, Karai Sándor, Markó Ferenc,
Móker József , Pálinkás Zsolt, Sárhidai Gyula, Sőregi Zoltán,
Szollár János, Tarr Péter for their photo collection
and a special thanks to FORTEPAN.

Hungarian Armored Forces in World War II • Péter Mujzer • First edition • LUBLIN 2017

© All English Language Rights Reserved. With the exception of quoting brief passages for the purposes of review, no part of this publication may be reproduced without prior written permission from the Publisher. Nazwa serii zastrzeżona w UP RP • **ISBN 978-83-65437-65-5**

Editors: **Péter Mujzer** • Photo: **Bonhardt Attila, Éder Miklós, Fortepan, Karai Sándor, Markó Ferenc, Móker József, Mujzer Péter, Pálinkás Zsolt, Sárhidai Gyula, Sőregi Zoltán, Széplaki Gábor, Szollár János, Tarr Péter** • Coloured original photos: **Deák Tamás** • Photo caption: **Péter Mujzer** • Color profiles: **Arkadiusz Wróbel (Color profiles based on Deák Tamás art works)** • Line drawings: **Bajtos Iván** • Design: **KAGERO STUDIO, Łukasz Maj**

KAGERO Publishing
Akacjowa 100, Turka, os. Borek, 20-258 Lublin 62, Poland, phone/fax: (+48) 81 501 21 05
www.kagero.pl • e-mail: kagero@kagero.pl, marketing@kagero.pl
w w w . k a g e r o . p l

INTRODUCTION

Since 1699, Hungary had been part of the Austrian Empire, ruled by the Habsburg dynasty. In 1848/49, the Hungarians staged an uprising seeking their independence, and although the attempt was crushed by the Austrians, it resulted in 1867 that Hungary being granted equal status with Austria. The empire became the dual monarchy of Austria and Hungary. It was known as the kaiserliche und königliche (k. und k.) Monarchy. The kaiserliche part referred to the Imperial throne of Austria, while the königliche part referred to the Royal throne of Hungary.

At the end of the First World War, Hungary, as a member of the k. und k. Monarchy, ended up on the losing side. Her army disintegrated and her armaments were either taken over or destroyed by the victorious Allied nations. In the autumn of 1919, after the failure of a short-lived Soviet-style republic, a new Hungarian National Army was organised under French supervision. This army was led by a former k. und k. admiral, the highest-ranking native Hungarian military officer, Admiral Miklós Horthy, who was later (in 1920) to become Regent of Hungary, ruling in place of the deposed Habsburgs. Hungary never officially renounced its status as a monarchy, and effectively the nation remained a monarchy without a king until the end of the Second World War.

After WWI, Hungary was in a very critical situation. In 1920 the Allied Powers gave the Hungarian delegation their conditions for peace. This agreement, the Treaty of Trianon, was very similar to the one already imposed on Germany at Versailles, and a French General was later to state that the only result was a twenty year long cease-fire, nothing more. The peace conditions for Hungary reduced the area of the country from 282,000 square kilometres to 93,000 square kilometres and the population from 18 million to 9.5 million. Thus 3,263,000 Hungarians became citizens of foreign countries under hostile administrations. The provisions of the Treaty of Trianon reduced Hungary's 1914 industrial base by about 80%.

The Treaty of Trianon was a huge shock for the whole society. The Treaty has left a never ending scar on the Hungarian national consciousness. Everybody was affected, at least

Admiral Miklós Horthy, governor of Hungary on the peak of his power, receiving the report of his general during the official ceremony of the re-conquest of Transylvania at Marosvásárhely, in 1940. Next to him are visible, his aide du camp Maj. Gen. Lajos Keresztes-Fischer and the commander of the Royal Guard Unit, Maj. Gen. Károly Lázár. [Fortepan 09354]

emotional by the harsh conditions of the Treaty. Hungary had lost his imperial status and was reduced to a small country surrounded by hostile states.

Military Conditions of the Peace Treaty

The main military aspects of the peace treaty were as follows: Military service based on contracted soldiers, conscription was forbidden, and the army was to consist of no more than 35,000 men. Training of officers was restricted and the existence of a General Staff was prohibited. The formation of Gendarmerie, Police and Frontier Guard units was also curbed. All war ma-

5/8.M 8 cm AA-Artillery gun mounted on a Rába V.R. truck with strange camouflage and its crew still wearing the old 17M helmet. [Szollár János]

Cyclist platoon of the Ludovika Academy receive the order for training in early 30s. The rifles not attached to the bicycle frame instead of carry by the cadets. [Mujzer Péter]

Despatch rider in great coat is on a BSA motorbike in the 30s, the motorbike has a metal Motorised Branch sign on the mudguard under the light. [Mujzer Péter]

gunpowder. Apart from the framework given for the Armed Forces, the production or purchase of arms was generally made impossible. These draconian measures were intended to ensure that the security of the newly created successor states, Romania, Czechoslovakia and Yugoslavia, would be guaranteed, and to maintain the decisive allied military supremacy in the region.

It was evident from the very beginning that the nation would not follow these dictates, if it could be circumvented. Hungarian foreign policy made no secret that its aim was to regain the lost territories. Hungary signed the Treaty of Trianon on 4th June 1920 because it had no other alternative, but her goal was to invalidate the Treaty as soon as possible.

The Hungarian Armed Forces between the Wars

The Hungarian Army, due to the limitations imposed by the Trianon Treaty, was unable to protect the country. The available manpower was just enough to maintain internal security in accordance with the requirements of the Little Entente states: Czechoslovakia, Yugoslavia, and Romania. The basic formation of the Army became the mixed brigade, of which seven were organised. The Army also formed four cavalry/hussar Regiments and a few support units to arrive at the permitted total of 35.000 men.

The plan was to establish a flexible, powerful and not too expensive basic formation, which later could be used as the cadre for expansion to a larger army. The mixed brigades were composed of two infantry regiments, one artillery and one

terials, which could be found, were confiscated. The existence or use of guns larger than l05mm calibre, tanks and all heavy armaments was forbidden.

Military aviation and the production of warplanes were prohibited. All warships, except for six small river patrol boats, were forbidden, as was the production and export of guns and

Mechanised artillery battery with 31. M 10,5cm guns were one of the most modern artillery pieces of the Hungarian Army during the war. [Mujzer Péter]

4

AA unit is on training with 29. M Bofors 8 cm gun at Hajmáskér firing range in the 30s. The AA units were concealed, due to the Peace Treaty's regulation. That is why this unit belonged to the River Forces and the crews were dressed in River Forces' uniform. [Mujzer Péter]

A 15/31. M 7,5cm cavalry gun decorated with garlands and children, the modernised version of the 15. M mountain gun, it was towed by six horses to keep up with the cavalry and belonged to the regimental gun batteries. [Mujzer Péter]

Cyclist is in full summer marching order, bicycle packed according to the regulation. The already heavy bicycle was overloaded and the movement was difficult in mountainous terrain. [Mujzer Péter]

cyclist battalion, mortar and cavalry companies plus support units. Seven brigades were organised and were allocated to seven military districts within Hungary. However, the Hungarian government and military leadership recognised that these units could not protect Hungary. Following Germany's example, the Hungarian Army began to organise secret units, and to conceal war materials, in direct violation of the dictates of the Trianon Treaty. These extra units were hidden in the branches of the State Police, Customs Service, Gendarmerie and other non-combatant governmental and non-governmental entities such as shipping companies and airlines.

Despatch rider poses on a Puch motorcycle, the soldier wears the two pieces leather protective suit and the Italian style crash helmet. [Mujzer Péter]

The Hungarian Army had a huge number of well-trained officers, both professionals and reservists, who had gained valuable experience in the k. und k. Army in WWI. There were many who wished to serve, but in an army that was only one tenth the size of the k. und k. Army, only a small percent of them could serve in true military units, while the rest were passed to non-military, governmental duties.

The armaments originated from the k. und k. Army, and as such were much worn due to their extensive use during WWI. Forbidden heavy artillery pieces, armoured trains and other prohibited weapons were concealed all around Hungary in civilian stores, cellars or simply dug under the earth to conceal them from the Allied Military Committee. The Hungarian State Railways (MÁV) played a major role in this hid and seek game. Train loads of forbidden materials were transported all around Hungary. Unfortunately, the result of these improper storage conditions was that the majority of the weapons, ammunitions were damaged, rusted and unsuitable for use in case of war.

The output of Hungarian military industries was either confiscated by Romanian forces in 1920, or destroyed by the Allied Military Committee. The greatest problem of the Hungarian Army was its very poor financial condition, which created a serious obstacle to modernisation and enlargement. Starting in 1927, the pressure from the Allied Committee lessened, and the constant supervision ended.

Hungarian Diplomacy

Hungarian diplomacy worked to form a close Italian, Austrian and Hungarian relationship in the late 1920s and early 1930s, to avoid isolation and to try to create a better position for Hungary among the European nations. In 1927 Hungary signed a treaty of co-operation with Italy. In the mid-1930s the international political situation changed. Germany had invalidated the Treaty of Versailles and begun to build up a modern regular army. To the Hungarians, Germany seemed to present the opportunity for a good alliance, perhaps providing the only support that Hungary could expect in its quest to recoup her losses of WWI.

As previously stated, Hungary's main aim was to regain her lost territories, especially those where Hungarians lived as

35. M Ansaldo tankette platoon belonged to the 14. Bicycle Battalion took part in the occupation of Transylvania. The tankette platoons' has its own unit sign; in that case it is the white skulk with dagger. [Mujzer Péter]

a majority. However the military leadership had no illusions about the real potential of the Hungarian Armed Forces. That is why Hungary first focused on a political solution and looked at a military solution as secondary. A comparison of the strengths of the Little Entente's forces with the Hungarian Army reveals the significant differences in size and armaments.

In November of 1938, after the Munich Agreement the Hungarians, due to the Vienna Arbitrage regained Upper-Hungary from Czechoslovakia.

The Hungarians occupied Carpathian-Ukraine by force against the Slovakians in March 1939. The next step was the conflict with Romania for Transylvania. The tension between Hungary and Romania reached a peak in summer of 1940, owing to Romania's failure to respond to Hungarian claims to the disputed area of Transylvania. The possibility of a conflict was against the German interest, they intervened and the second Vienna Arbitrage decided that one part of Transylvania was given back to Hungary. The last step on the road to regain the lost territory was the participation in the Balkan Campaign against Yugoslavia. In this case, Hungarians gained again former Hungarian territories by force and casualties.

Exchange for the German political and military support Hungary had to pay dearly to the Third Reich. In November 1940 Hungary signed an alliance agreement with the Germans which gave extra rights for them.

The Germans did not plane to involve directly the Hungarians to the Barbarossa Campaign. Original the Hungarian role was to be a secure communication line, logistic, supply base. But on 26 of June 1941 three unidentified twin-engine bombers attacked a Hungarian city, Kassa (*Kosice*) not far from the border. In same afternoon different targets were low-level attacked by Soviet aircrafts. These, probably unwilling incidents were enough for the Hungarian Government as "casus belli" to involve in to the WWII. It was the output of a strange race between Hungary and Romania for keeping the status quo and for the alliance and goodwill of the Third Reich.

The Hungarians took part in the Eastern Front operations in 1941- 45.

The Hungarians have became an unreliable ally after Stalingrad and tried to seek the opportunity to left the Axis. It generated the German reaction, the temporary military occupation of Hungary and the replacement of the government by a pro German one from 19th of March 1944. However Admiral Horthy remained in position. The majority of the population looked at on the Germans rather as brothers in arms than enemies.

A significant Hungarian Jewish population lived in Hungary. Their double faced status was ended after the German occupation in March 1944.

The Hungarian government already proclaimed the so called "Jewish Acts" in 1938-1944. These legal and administrative rules made their life hard and difficult. Their businesses were taken over by the Hungarian State. The Jews were down graded to second class citizens. In 1941 the Hungarian government deported 20 000 so called non Hungarian citizens from Hungary to Kamenets-Podolsky area. These peoples were executed by the German Einsatzkommandos and their Ukrainian allies. The male, military aged Jews were called into labour units. Due to the cruel treatment, a lot of Jewish men were killed and lost with the labour units on the Eastern Front.

Mechanised column take part in an exercise, in the foreground is a Krupp Protze L. H. 143 truck with ex-Polish fuel trailer. [Fortepan 38976, Csorba Dániel]

Early armoured cars belonged to the RUISK. In the foreground is the Rába V.P., next is the 29. M Vickers. The third vehicle is a truck armed with the 07. M Schwarzlose machine gun. [Szollár János]

On the other hand the majority of them could live better than any other Jewish in the occupied Europe until 1944. After the German occupation their fate was sealed. Most of the Hungarian Jews were deported with a willing Hungarian administrative assistance to the German operated concentration camps. During the war 410-460 000 Hungarian Jews perished, the total casualty of Hungary was 830-950 000 men.

In the summer of 1944 the Red Army arrived to the Hungarian border. The war stepped on the Hungarian soil with its full force and brutality. On 15th of October 1944 Regent Horthy, who had continued his secret negotiations with the Allies, proclaimed an armistice. The armistice was badly organised on military and political level. The Germans were well informed and well prepared. Horthy was arrested and enforced to hand over his power to Ferenc Szállasi and the "Arrow Cross" movement. Who was pledged to continue the war.

The Enlargement of the Hungarian Army

During the secret rearmament, the Hungarian Army initially concentrated on enlarging the personnel strength and in building up a supply of the equipment forbidden by the Treaty of Trianon. Starting in the mid-thirties, Hungary had a chance to purchase weapons and armaments from Italy and Germany and from neutral countries such as Sweden and Switzerland. The home based military industry was also enlarged in accordance with the overall economic situation. By 1938 the Hungarian Army had seven mixed brigades, one cavalry division, (two hussar brigades,) an aviation brigade, an experimental motorised group and the River Forces. Under the direct command of the Chief of the General Staff were two heavy artillery battalions, four A/A artillery battalions, one signal battalion, one chemical warfare battalion, a mechanised transport regiment and an armoured group.

The total strength was 85,000 men, two and half times more than permitted by the peace treaty. 1938 brought a decisive change in the Hungarian Army's situation and development. Relying on the German-Italian alliance, and backed by the Polish and Austrian governments, the Hungarian Government revealed its rearmament program.

On March of 5, 1938, Prime Minister Kálmán Darányi announced his government's 1 billion Pengő rearmament program which, disregarding political and financial barriers, was aimed at accelerating the rebuilding of the national defence system within 3-5 years. This rearmament program dealt mainly with the enlargement of the mobile troops and the air force. In the 1936-1937 budget year, the national budget of Hungary was 4.417 million Pengő (almost $1.3 million with an exchange rate at that time of 1 USD equalling 3.40 Pengő).

This plan provided a boost not only to the army but also to the country as a whole, generating many new industries and extra profits for the military industry. Recognition by the Little Entente states that, from their point of view, the international situation had deteriorated led them to negotiate an equal rearmament pact with Hungary, which was signed in a small Yugoslavian town, Bled on August 22, 1938. As of this time, Hungary's rearmament was legal. However, there still remained the problem of the impoverished state of the nation.

After the signature of the Bled equal rearmament treaty, Hungary speeded up the enlarging of its army. The former mixed brigades were expanded to form infantry corps, each with three infantry brigades. The final enlargement plan, called the "Huba Plan", called for the establishment of the following units by 1942:

25 infantry brigades, each consisting of two infantry regiments
1 cavalry and two armoured divisions
2 mountain brigades
1 frontier guard brigade
1 river forces brigade
2 air force brigades

CHAPTER I

Hungarian Armoured Troops in the Early Years

As already mentioned in the introduction, the Treaty of Trianon prohibited any kind of armoured vehicle or armoured troops for the Hungarian Army. However, the leadership of the Army recognised the importance of this new branch and equipment and remembered the successes that had been achieved by the use of armoured trains and armoured cars during WWI.

The first real tanks of the Hungarian Army were purchased from the stock of the former German Mackensen Army via Sweden, in the spring of 1920. The fourteen LK II tanks arrived on barges, shipped along the River Danube.

The contract for the purchase was concluded before the Trianon Treaty was signed, but the shipping of the tanks was

Barracks of the RUISK at Budapest in the early 30s. The 29M Crossley armoured car seen with a troop carrier truck. [Szollár János]

29M Crossley armoured car is on exercise, the crew already wear the regular army uniform. [Szollár János]

done in secret, with the tanks covered in wheat and the barges anchoring at a civilian (rather than military) port facility on the River Danube. Due to the peace treaty, Hungary could not put these light tanks into service. The tanks were transported by rail all around Hungary to avoid inspection by the Allied Military Commission

RUISK

The first real progress made was the establishment of the Police Training School (RUISK), which became the cadre for the new Hungarian armoured branch. Faced with the limitations of the Treaty of Trianon, it was normal practice to hide secret military units under the guise of various paramilitary and governmental services. The RUISK was formed on May 5, 1924 as a central reserve and training unit of the Hungarian State Police, but it also served as a cover agency for military units.

The RUISK had an armoured car section of 2-3 armour-plated trucks with a primitive turret. The main aim of this unit was to carry out experimental work for the new armoured branch, to formulate tactics, to examine the use of different type of tanks and armoured cars, and to define ideal formations and organisations. The available vehicles were too few and too rudimentary for this job. However, in 1927 the Allied Military Committee left Hungary and this opened up new opportunities to the Hungarian Army. At first the armoured unit of the RUISK was expanded to the size of an armoured group, and equipment

that had been hidden for years from the eyes of the Allies was now gathered and deployed in military depots.

With the special permission of the Entente, Hungary purchased two Armstrong-Vickers armoured cars for use by the Police. Later, various civilian trucks were purchased and covered with armour plating, but except for the trucks made by Krupp and Crossley, they were unable to carry the weight of the armour. At least two Crossley armoured cars with two machine-guns in their turrets and one Krupp armoured radio car produced by the end of the 1920s. The RUISK had seven different armoured cars in 1929, but these were able to be used only for police and training tasks.

The order of battle of 1930 contained an armoured group with one armoured car and one light tank company, equipped with eight armoured cars, one radio car and five LK II tanks. The need for training increased, and so twelve Fiat F2 cars were converted to armoured cars and seven BMW cars were covered with canvas to form dummy tanks in 1930-32. Due to its good relationship with the Italian military, the Hungarian Army received five Fiat 3000B light tanks, with the shipping being done in secret. They were assigned to the light tank company. In 1932 a Carden-Lloyd tankette arrived in Hungary, but after trials no more were purchased due to the poor technical performance of the vehicle.

The lack of materiel for the armoured forces notwithstanding, the General Staff was able to clearly define the conditions and strategic requirements for using the armoured troops. The

Soldiers of the Experimental Motorised Group stand in summer light weighted uniform in front of a Rába truck. [Markó Ferenc]

The Tankette Company of the 2. Reconnaissance Battalion assembled somewhere in Transylvania in 1940. The first two 35. M FIAT Ansaldo have commander's observation cupola, invented by the Hungarians. [Szollár János]

The 1. Cavalry Brigade's units took part in the occupation of Carpathian-Ukraine in March of 1939. The white standing triangle symbolised the 1. Cavalry Armoured Battalion's troops. [Bonhardt Attila]

strategy was to use the mobile units independently. In theory, the main power of the mobile troops lay with the tank units, equipped with tankettes and light tanks. The intention was for each tank company to have eleven light tanks and five tankettes. However, in reality, available resources limited the companies to just five Fiat 3000B light tanks, one Carden Lloyd tankette and seven armoured cars. In the early 1930s the biggest problem was that the states friendly to Hungary (Germany and Italy) lacked proper armoured vehicles, and the Entente states refused to sell Hungary these materials.

The Italian Connection

The turning point for the Hungarian armoured forces was an Italian offer to deliver the new CV-33 FIAT Ansaldo tankette to Hungary. In June 1934 the Military Technical Institute tested the CV-33 tankette and advised that these should be put into service. The Hungarian Army ordered 150 tankettes from Turin and put them into service as the 35. M FIAT Ansaldo tankette in 1935. The last 35. M tankettes arrived in December 1936.

The battle order of 1936 called for each mixed brigade to include an armoured company with 35. KM Ansaldo tankettes; these were classified as "automobile companies". However, since these companies had never been established as separate units, the 150 tankettes were placed into storage at Hajmáskér and Örkénytábor. Two training units were organised at these locations, one with ten and the other with five tankettes. The remainder was kept in storage during peacetime.

New Sources

In 1936 some new sources opened up for the Hungarian Army to obtain new armoured techniques and licenses. The Swedish Landsverk Factory offered Hungary the license to build the L-60 light tank. Germany offered the Pz.Kpfw. IA, but the Hungarians were not satisfied by this light, underpowered and under-armed tankette.

Next to Italy, Sweden was ready to sell military equipment and license to Hungary. The L-60 was a typical light tank of the beginning of war, and was put in service as 38. M Toldi tank in Hungary. [Mujzer Péter]

Cadets practice with factory fresh 38. M Toldi tank at Budapest, Ludovika Academy. [Fortepan 43938, Ludovika]

Factory fresh 39. M Csaba armoured cars in September 1940 Transylvania. The front vehicle has the number plate Pc.118, the armoured cars painted in three tones camouflage, no military insignia visible. [Fortepan 38969]

In the summer of 1938 the L-60 and the Hungarian-invented V-4 underwent competitive test trials; due to the overall good performance of the L-60, this model was selected.

The Ministry of Defence placed orders for it, designating it as the 38. M Toldi light tank, and the MAVAG and Ganz Factories purchased the licence rights and started mass production. For the reconnaissance battalions, the Manfred Weiss factory offered a light armoured car, which was being produced for export. After trial manoeuvres it was found to be an absolutely perfect armoured car, approved by the Military Technical Institute, and it was put into service as the 39. M Csaba armoured car in 1939.

Organisation and Equipment of the Armoured Units

The first mechanised unit of the Hungarian Army, the Experimental Motorised Group, was established in 1932. It also had one light tank and one armoured car company. In 1938 the newly created motorised rifle brigades each had one (armoured) reconnaissance battalion. The reconnaissance battalion of the 2nd Brigade was the first true armour unit of the Hungarian Army with one – one armoured car, tankette and motorised rifle company. The strength of the unit was based on the 3rd and 4th Tankette Companies and on the armoured cars of the Experimental Mechanised Group. The cavalry brigades also each received a tankette company.

The Hungarian version of the Swedish L-62 was the 40. M Nimród A/A-AT self-propelled vehicle. Test trial of the freshly made 40. M Nimróds was done with military and factory staff. [Szollár János]

Later, the armoured units of the cavalry brigades were enlarged to battalion size similar to the armoured battalions of the motorised brigades, consisting of one company each of light tanks (38. M Toldi), tankettes (35. M Ansaldo) and armoured cars (39. M Csaba). The companies had 16 vehicles; three platoons each with 5 armoured vehicles plus the company commander's vehicle.

A Hungarian Army delegation visited Poland shortly after the Wehrmacht's victorious campaign, where they recognised the importance of close co-operation between the mobile-armoured formations and the air force. They saw this combination as the ultimate device of a modern war. The delegation concluded that an independent, not-subordinated, corps-size mobile unit would be the decisive element on a modern battlefield.

Based on their recommendations the two cavalry and two motorised rifle brigades were organised as the I Mobile Corps in the autumn of 1940. The commanders of the mobile troops expressed an urgent need for tank battalions, mobile anti-tank and A/A defence units. The Ministry of Defence purchased a new self propelled A/A-AT armoured vehicle, the L-62 (40. M Nimród) from Landsverk in 1939. The greatest problem was the lack of medium and heavy tanks. Because of the war, Hungary could not purchase these from Germany and Italy. The only solution was a former Czechoslovakian medium tank, the T-21, which was later produced under licence as the 40. M Turán tank.

As of December 1940, the Mobile Corps order of battle was re-organised following the delivery of the new armoured vehicles (38. M Toldi and 39. M Csaba). The new plan also included the 40. M Nimród and 40. M Turán armoured vehicles, even though they were not yet being produced. One cyclist battalion (9th and 11th) of each motorised rifle brigade was converted into a tank battalion. The tank battalion, theoretically consisting of three light and one medium tank companies, each had 23 tanks plus the battalion staff with three light tanks and one medium tank and two A/A-AT companies, each with six 40. M Nimróds. The new, reorganised battalions officially were named as 9th and 11th Cyclist-Tank Battalion. During the transition period the battalions consisted of battalion staff, sapper, signals, maintenance platoons and 2-2 light tank and cyclist companies.

Due to the lack of light tanks, the motorised and cavalry brigades transferred their Toldi companies to the newly created tank battalions, and the cavalry brigades received the tankette companies of the motorised rifle brigades. The armoured cavalry battalions released half of their 38. M Toldis. Nine light tanks remained with the battalions to reinforce the 35. M Ansaldo companies. These complicated changes resulted in a motorised rifle brigade having one tank battalion and one reconnaissance battalion. On June 20, 1941 the 9th and 11th Battalions each received 18 38. M Toldi light tanks from the central reserve. The tank battalions had two companies of light tanks; each equipped with 18 Toldi tanks and the replacement/training unit with 8 Toldi tanks.

The reconnaissance battalion had one-one armoured car, motorcycle, motorised rifle and staff company with 39. M Csaba armoured cars and 38. M Botond trucks. The cavalry brigade had a single armoured battalion with one armoured car company (39. M Csaba) and two tankette companies (35. M Ansaldo). The tankette companies were each reinforced by

Reconnaissance battalion's units wait for marching order. Between the Ansaldo and Toldi companies is a Mercedes G5 staff car. [Mujzer Péter]

1. Armoured Cavalry Battalion mixed armoured vehicles, Toldis and Ansaldos move on an exercise. The 38. M Toldi tanks bearing the white Turul unit sign in 1941. [Szollár János]

one 38. M Toldi platoon. The 6 cyclist battalions (10th, 12th, 13th, 14th, 15th, 16th) subordinated to the Mobile Corps also had a tankette platoon with 6-6 35. M Ansaldos.

This new organisation was completed immediately prior to Hungary becoming involved in the Barbarossa Campaign. With the start of the campaign in the summer of 1941, the Mobile Corps with its Csaba, Toldi and Ansaldo armoured units was deployed into the Ukraine.

The next reorganisation of the armoured forces took place in October 1941, while the Mobile Corps was still fighting in Ukraine. The idea was to form an armoured division, the 2nd with one tank and one motorised rifle brigades. It based on the German armoured division's order of battle. The Mobile Corps was re-organised with the new unit, the 2nd Armoured Division, which was made up of:

2nd Armoured Brigade, (newly created)
2nd Motorised Brigade, (already in existence)
51st A/A-AT Battalion (newly created)

The 1st Motorised Rifle Brigade, (already in existence) was also belonged to the Mobile Corps.

The 2nd Armoured Brigade had four battalions, 1/I, 2/I, 3/I, 4/I, which were organised from the 10th, 12th, 13th, 16th, Cyclist Battalions. The 31st Independent Battalion was organised from the 9th Tank Battalion, while the 32nd Independent Battalion was created from the 11th Tank Battalion.

The newly created battalions were equipped only with 38. M Toldis, since the 40. M Turán and 40. M Nimród armoured vehicles were still in production. The tank battalion had three companies, initially two mediums and one light, later three medium companies. The A/A-AT battalion had three companies of 40. M Nimróds.

According to this plan the tank battalions of the rifle brigades (31st and 32nd) remained with the brigades. They have a reduced strength of two light companies (2x22 Toldi tanks) and one A/A-AT company (6 Nimród). At the same time, the Hungarian war industry had received an enormous order to produce new armoured vehicles; 38. M Toldi, 39. M Csaba, 40. M Nimród and medium 40. M Turán vehicles, plus the new modified heavy 41. M Turán tank.

In the meantime armoured units of the Mobile Corps were continuing to fight on the Eastern Front but due to the difficult terrain their casualties were mounting and the damaged vehicles were sent for repair to the factories. This explains why in 1942 the Hungarian Army had in its order of battle only one tank regiment and two independent tank battalions but no real armoured units.

Armoured Cavalry Battalion's companies assembling in a Transylvanian town square. The Ansaldo tankette, Toldi light tank and Csaba armoured car companies forming line behind each other. [Mujzer Péter]

Units of the 2. Armoured Division paraded at Kecskemét in mid 40s. That time the Ansaldo tankettes were used for training without armament. In front of the Botond truck is a Puch 350 GS motorcycle. [Mujzer Péter]

In 1942 Hungary sent its 2nd Army to Russia, but due to the lack of Hungarian vehicles its armoured division was equipped with German tanks. The unit was designated the 1st Armoured Field Division and it was an ad hoc formation, not included in the order of battle. The 1st Armoured Field Division was created from the following units:

1st Motorised Rifle Brigade (excluding the 31st Independent Tank Battalion),

51st A/A-AT Battalion from the 2nd Armoured Division,

1st Reconnaissance Battalion from the 1st Motorised Rifle Brigade

30th Tank Regiment (with German tanks and crews from different Hungarian armoured units).

The 38. M Toldi tanks for the 1st Armoured Field Division were amassed from the armoured cavalry battalions. The division had one tank unit, the 30th Tank Regiment with two battalions, each battalion with one heavy and two medium companies of Pz. IV and 38(t) tanks.

The 1st Reconnaissance Battalion had one motorised rifle company (12 light machine guns, 2 light mortars, 2 anti-tank rifles), one motorcycle company (12 light machine guns, 2 anti-tank rifles), one anti-tank gun company (four 36. M 37mm, two PAK38 50mm anti-tank guns), one armoured car company (14 39. M Csaba armoured cars).

The 51st A/A-AT Battalion had three companies, with 18 40. M Nimród A/A-AT vehicles.

The division also had the 1st Motorised Rifle Brigade with three rifle battalions and one- one motorcycle, movement control company, one-one signal and pioneer platoon. The motorised rifle battalions had three rifle companies (each company had 12 light machine guns, 2 light mortars and 2 anti-tank rifles), one heavy weapons company (12 machine guns, 4 mortars), and one anti-tank gun company (four 36. M 37mm, two PAK38 50mm guns), as well as sapper and signals platoons. In addition, the division had two artillery battalions, the 1st and 5th with 3 batteries, each of four 37. M 105mm howitzers. The II A/A Artillery Battalion had two batteries, each with four 29. M 80mm Bofors guns. Finally, the division had a signal battalion, pioneer and movement control company, and miscellaneous support units.

CHAPTER II

Final organisation of the Armoured Forces

Based on combat experiences during 1941, the General Staff of the Hungarian Army modified the organisation of the Mobile Brach. It became clear that the deployment of different kinds of troops (mechanised, cavalry and cyclist) in one unit was not satisfactory.

40. M Nimród A/A-AT vehicle is on a driving exercise. The spare fuel drum transported in the turret. The military insignia is missing. [Fortepan 43972, Ludovika]

41. M Turán heavy tanks, pride of the Armoured Forces lined in a garage of the Automobile Depot in 1943. The weapons covered in protective canvas. [Fortepan 72451, Lissák Tivadar]

Armoured Cavalry Units

The cavalry units were removed from the Mobile Corps order of battle. The two cavalry brigades were disbanded in October 1942. Three hussar regiments were organised into the 1st Cavalry Division in 1942. The armoured cavalry battalions of the cavalry brigades were also disbanded, and a reconnaissance and a cavalry tank battalion were formed for the division. The reconnaissance battalion got the 39. M Csaba armoured cars and the tank battalion got the new 40. M and 41. M Turán tanks in 1943.

The reconnaissance battalion was numbered the 3rd and was stationed at Szilágysomlyó. The tank battalion was numbered the 1st based at Zenta. It had three medium, one heavy and one staff companies.

The armoured cars of the two former armoured cavalry battalions were concentrated in the new 3rd Reconnaissance Battalion, although it did not gain full strength until 1944. The 15th Cyclist Battalion also belonged to the 1st Cavalry Division.

Armoured Divisions

In October 1942 the Mobile Corps was converted into the I Armoured Corps consisting of the Corps' HQ, 1st and 2nd Armoured Divisions, and the 1st Armoured Signal Battalion (three signal companies). The organisation of the new armoured divisions consisted of one tank and one motorised rifle regiment, with three battalions of each plus one reconnaissance battalion, one engineer battalion, a signal battalion, an A/A artillery battalion and a A/A-AT battalion, three mechanised artillery battalions, plus supply units.

Six tank battalions were organised into two tank regiments. The battalions had two medium and two heavy companies and one staff and one supply company. The planning for future re-organisation called for the creation of a total of four armoured divisions, so the battalions were numbered accordingly. When it became clear that these four divisions could not be created, due to limited industrial capacity, the 2/I Battalion was renumbered 1/III and the 4/I Battalion was renumbered 3/III.

The motorised rifle regiments and battalions had the same organisation as they had in 1942/43, except for the new Nimród AA platoons, which were attached to the battalions. The 1st Armoured Division (newly created) received the 1st Tank Regiment from the 2nd Armoured Brigade (2nd Armoured Division). The Regiment was made up of the 1/I, 2/I, 1/II (31st Independent) Battalions. The 2nd Armoured Division, in existence from October 1941, included the newly created 3rd Tank Regiment with the 3/I, 4/I and 3/II (32nd Independent) Battalions On paper, an armoured division was to have the following armoured vehicles:

66 heavy tank 41. M Turán
114 medium tank 40. M Turán
82 light tank 38. M Toldi
42 A/A-AT vehicle 40. M Nimród
14 armoured car 39. M Csaba

The tank regiment consisted of one of each staff, sapper and maintenance company. The staff company had three 40. M Turán tanks (2 commander, 1 normal vehicles) plus a reconnaissance platoon with 5 x 38. M Toldi light tanks. The battalion staff company had a similar complement with the addition of one Nimród platoon equipped with one 38. M Toldi light tank and 4 x 40. M Nimród A/A-AT vehicles. The heavy companies were equipped with 11 x 41. M heavy Turán tanks plus a reconnaissance platoon with 5 x 38. M Toldi tanks. The medium companies had 17 x 40. M medium Turán tanks and 5 x 38. M Toldi light tanks at the reconnaissance platoon. The tank battalion also had a supply company.

The motorised rifle battalions each had one platoon of 4 x 40. M Nimród.

Prototype of the command version Turán tank was equipped with two R-4 and one R-5/a radio. In return the main gun was dummy one. [Éder Miklós]

The A/A-AT battalion had one 38. M Toldi light tank for the battalion staff, and 6 x 40. M Nimróds plus one 38. M Toldi tank for each of the three companies. The reconnaissance battalion had one 39. M Csaba armoured car for the battalion staff and 13 x 39. M Csaba armoured cars for the armoured car company. In 1943 the armoured units were located as follows:

1st Armoured Division
1 /I Tank Battalion, Esztergom
1 /II Tank Battalion, Jászberény
1 /III Tank battalion, Rétság
2nd Armoured Division
3/I Tank Battalion, Cegléd
3/II Tank Battalion, Kecskemét
3/III Tank Battalion, Kiskunhalas

Assault artillery

According to the official terminology the assault artillery did not belonged to the Mobile/Armoured Branch. It was organised, inspected and crewed mainly by artillery men and officers. On the other hand they fought with armoured vehicles. Their history is inseparable from the Armoured Troops.

The Hungarian Army organised assault gun battalions which it was planned to equip with Hungarian-made Zrínyi assault guns/howitzers. On October 1, 1943, the 1st and the 10th Assault Gun Battalions and the 2nd-8th Assault Gun Training Cadres were formed. These cadres were organised for training crews for the battalions, and in April 1944 these cadres were converted into assault gun battalions. By this time, training had started with

Maintenance of the 40. M Turán medium tanks carry out by the crew. The turret side hatch is well visible on the picture. [Szollár János]

Armament of a motorised rifle battalion is on display in 1944. The collection consisted of 40. M Nimród A/A-AT vehicles, PAK-40 anti-tank gun. The parading officers wear cavalry boots with spur. [Mujzer Péter]

Toldi and Turán tanks. The 1st Assault Gun Battalion had 10 x 41. M heavy Turán and 10 x 38. M Toldi light tanks, and the 2nd, 8th Assault Gun Training Cadres received 7 heavy 41. M Turán tanks.

The assault gun battalions were organised under the eight infantry divisions and carried the number of the infantry divisions: 7th ,10th , 13th , 16th , 20th , 24th , 25th, except for the 1st Assault Gun Battalion which was assigned to the 6th Infantry Division. Following the German pattern, the battalions consisted of three batteries each with 10 assault guns plus a staff battery. The strength of an assault gun battalion was 741 men, 31 assault gun, 120 trucks and 70 motorcycles. During the last part of the war, some of the assault gun units were equipped with German materials. The 1st and 10th Assault Gun Battalions were equipped with Zrínyi assault howitzers. The 16th and 20th battalion (3 batteries) received Hetzers and the 7th Battalion received the StuG III.

Reconnaissance Battalions

Following the new overall organisation, the Hungarian Army had eight first line infantry divisions (each with three infantry regiments) and each of them had one assault gun battalion and one reconnaissance battalion. Two different type reconnaissance battalion was organised, one for the new infantry divisions and one for the armoured and cavalry divisions.

The reconnaissance battalions belonging to the infantry divisions consisted of one company each of cavalry (hussars) and cyclists, and one platoon each of armoured cars (four 39. M Csaba), anti-tank guns (4 guns), mortar (4 mortars), signal and sapper. The armoured car platoons were rarely equipped with armoured cars due to the shortage of the 39. M Csaba armoured cars.

The two armoured divisions also had one reconnaissance battalions each, the 1st and 2nd. These were equipped with an armoured car company (13 x 39. M Csaba armoured cars), a motorised rifle company (12 light machine guns, 2 light mortars, 2 anti-tank rifles), a motorcycle company (12 light machine guns, 2 anti-tank rifles) and a staff company with signal, sapper, anti-tank gun (4 guns) and maintenance platoons.

The 1st Cavalry Division included the 3rd Reconnaissance Battalion with two armoured car companies (26 x 39. M Csaba armoured cars) and a staff company with signal, sapper, anti-tank gun (4 guns) and maintenance platoons.

The battalions were stationed as follows:
1st Reconnaissance Battalion, Budapest
2nd Reconnaissance Battalion, Kassa
3rd Reconnaissance Battalion, Szilágysomlyó

Independent Units

101st Motorised Chemical Warfare Battalion

The 101st Motorised Chemical Warfare Battalion was organised in 1938, and had a platoon of 35. M Ansaldos. The task of this battalion was to perform smoke screen and flame throwing activities, and to use combat gases and gas counter-measures against the enemy. Only two 35. M Ansaldos were equipped with trolleys for transporting smoke screen generators or flame-thrower liquid, but neither saw any action.

Guard Rifle Battalion

The Royal Hungarian Guard Rifle Battalion was organised to protect the Regent of Hungary, Admiral Miklós Horthy in 1943/44. The battalion was a well armed rifle unit, consisted of three rifles, one-one heavy weapons and armoured company. The traditional Guard Unit' strength was augmented by the Battalion's fire power. Their role was to protect the Admiral,

38. M Toldi light tank remains in service up to the end of the war. This tank belonged to the 1/II Tank Battalion at Jászberény. [Sőregi Zoltán]

The side view of the 40/43. M Zrínyi assault howitzer iron prototype is on the evaluation course in 1943. [Éder Miklós]

Factory fresh 39. M Csaba armoured car is at the Automobile Depot with dark green camouflage and late style military insignia in 1943, wait for the distribution to the Reconnaissance Forces. [Fortepan 72480, Lissák Tivadar]

Despatch rider is on a Puch GS 350 motorcycle in 1942. He wears the leather protective suit and Italian style crash helmet, armed with 31M carbine. [Fortepan 42973, Konok Tamás id]

his family, the government in case of any kind of hostile act. Original the armoured company was planned to equip with Turán tanks and Zrínyi assault guns.

Finally the Guard Rifle Battalion was supplied with three (according to other sources six) 40. M Nimród A/A-AT vehicles in July 1944. The platoon size unit was commanded by Capt. Bennó Festetics and was officially called as company. The crew were uniformed and equipped according to the Guard Rifle's standards.

The Nimrods were planned to use in A/A and infantry support roles around the Castle of Buda (Budapest). Upon arrival, one of the Nimrod had a technical brake down. It was towed into the yard of the Battalion's barracks and survived the siege of Budapest. The serviceable Nimrods were deployed out of Budapest during the autumn of 1944. The left behind Nimrod is the only existing WWII Hungarian armoured vehicles currently in Hungary.

Gendarmerie Forces

After the withdrawal of the 35. M Ansaldos from active duty, ten each of the remaining vehicles were given to the Police, Gendarmerie and to the Croatian Forces. These were supplied without armaments, and the new owners had to install any weapons.

In 1942 a gendarmerie battalion was formed at Galánta, which was responsible for internal security (against armed riots); it had three rifle companies, one bicycle company, one heavy weapons company and one armoured company. The 35. M Ansaldos were transferred to this unit. In 1944 the gendarmerie armoured company had 12 Ansaldo tankettes and one platoon of 39. M Csaba armoured cars. The police and gendar-

Motorcyclists of the 15. Bycicle Battalion stand in front of their BMW R75 sidecar motorbikes. They wear their protective leather suits according to the regulation. [Mujzer Péter]

The State Police has two 39. M Csaba armoured cars, the turret armament was reduced, and the 20mm anti-tank rifle was removed. The police armoured cars was painted dark blue, the turret had an extra search light. [Mujzer Péter]

merie Ansaldos were deployed and destroyed during the siege of Budapest in 1944/1945.

Police Forces

As of 1942, the mobile reserve of the State Police was also equipped with armoured vehicles. An armoured group of State Police was organised with ten 35. M Ansaldo tankettes and two (or five) 39. M Csaba armoured cars and a special storm detachment to keep internal order in the capital. The armoured car and tankett subunits lead by officers. The 39. M Csaba armoured car was just armed with the 8mm machinegun, the 20mm anti-tank rifle was removed. The 35. M Ansaldos were equipped with one 31. M light machine-gun instead of the military equipment. At the end of 1943, two Skoda 38(t) tank was subordinated to the Police Armoured Group with army crew. The Skoda tanks were deployed to guard the entrance of the ghetto of Budapest.

Officer Candidates are on training with 35. M Ansaldo tankettes and R/3 field radio in 1941. The cadets wear overalls and crash helmets. [Fortepan 43870, Ludovika]

Reserve officer conversion training course held in 1943 at Esztergomtábor. The officers explore the 40mm gun of the 40. M Turán tank. [Szollár János]

Replacement and Cadre Units

It was typical for each Hungarian formation, down to the level of battalion, to have a cadre unit. In the case of mobilisation, when the active unit was sent to the front the replacement unit remained at home. The replacement unit was responsible for the training of fresh crews and for sending them to the front as replacements.

At the end of the war replacement units were organised under each corps into replacement field infantry divisions with reduced staff and armament.

The mobile and armoured troops also had their own replacement units. These were assigned the same name and number of the active unit with the addition of the designation "replacement", for example, 1st Replacement Motorised Rifle Battalion.

The 1st Armoured Division had to hand over majority of its armament and equipment to the 2nd Armoured Division, when it was deployed to Galicia in spring of 1944. The 1st Armoured Division was removed from the official Battle of Order. But very soon it was mobilised again as the 1st Replacement Armoured Division. The official sources refer to it as the 1st Replacement Armoured Division or simply as the 1st Armoured Division.

The 1st and 2nd Replacement Motorised Rifle Regiments consisted of three-two weak battalions and were thrown into battle in October 1944, Hungary.

It should be noted, however, that these replacement units had very limited equipment. Nevertheless, at the end of the war the replacement units were sent into battle alongside the first line units. The replacement cadre system was part of the theoretical organisation of the Hungarian armoured forces during WWII; however the structure was never completed.

CHAPTER III

Training of Armoured Forces

Officer Training

Independent military education in Hungary dated back to the 19th Century. The Ludovika Military Academy was established for the training of native Hungarian officer candidates within the k. und k. Monarchy. After WWI the Ludovika trained officers for the Hungarian Armed Forces.

The curriculum at the Ludovika consisted of one year enlisted training at their respective branch of the candidates and three years long academic studies.

From 1939 a Mobile Warfare Group was organised for cavalry, cyclist, and armoured officer candidates. The Mobile Warfare Group consisted of one-one cavalry, cyclist and armoured companies. It was commanded by Col. Andor Magyary. The cadets of the I. - III. Years served at their respective companies.

In 1940 a separate class was organised for the armoured cadets.

The specialised training of the motorised rifles officers started in 1941. The motorised rifles differentiated from the normal infantry that they moved by vehicles, but fight on foot like the infantry troops. At the beginning the grenadier and jäger officers and men were retrained as motorised rifles.

When the cyclist battalions were converted into tank battalions their officers were also retrained as armoured ones.

Armoured Training

Officer's education

In the first years after WWI, due to the restrictions of the Trianon Treaty, the training of officers and enlisted men was done in secret. Initially training was carried out at the RUISK (Police Training School), where officers with different backgrounds (from different branches of the Armed Forces) were trained. They received on-the-job training, without any written instruction. In the early 1930s, the situation improved and regular training was introduced.

As of 1934 the Ludovika Military Academy began regular education of young armoured officer candidates. In the first year only four candidates began their training. Later the number of candidates was enlarged. At the same time reserve training for the armoured branch was started. An Armoured Class for professional officers was established at the Ludovika Military Academy in 1940.

The Ludovika Academy released 217 armoured officers from 1938 until 1944. Forty-six of them were killed in action during the war.

Firing exercise carry out with a 38. M Toldi light tank at Esztergom-tábor, training ground of the armoured and mechanised forces. The aiming system can be seen through the open turret hatch. [Mujzer Péter]

The Armoured Class of the Ludovika Academy had three-three 35. M Ansaldo tankettes, 39. M Csaba armoured cars three 40. M Turán tanks, ten 38. M Toldi light tanks and one 40. M Nimród A/A-AT vehicle in 1943-44.

The „Csaba Királyfi" Mobile Troops Cadet School was established at Marosvásárhely, where candidates received four years of military education and one year practical experience with the mobile troops, after which they were promoted to the rank of Ensign. The Cadet School had three Csaba armoured cars in 1943.

Because of the need to enlarge the armoured branch, many officers from other branches were converted to armoured forces personnel. These officers mostly came from other mobile troops, i.e. cavalry, motorised rifle, or cyclist units. As the cavalry and cyclist officers were senior in rank and age, they dominated the key command and staff positions. According to the view of the high ranking officers; the rule of engagement of the armoured, motorised rifle units was similar to their predecessors, the cavalry and cyclist. On the one hand, these commanders tactically were up to their task, but on the other hand sometimes they were lack of the technical background of how to operate a mechanised force.

According to the Hungarian system, conscripted personals with grammar school degree were entitled to serve and train as reserve officers. During the first year they were trained to be reserve officer candidates at their units. Every regiment had its own "one year volunteers' school". The officer candidates were trained to be troop or platoon commander at their regiment. At the end of this one year course they were promoted to the rank of officer candidate sergeant. During the next conscripted year they served as platoon commander. Later on they were several times recall, for short periods to the Army and were promoted to reserve ensigns or 2nd Lt. The constant lack of manpower at the Officer Corps allowed reserve officers and officer candidates to apply to the professional Officer Corps. Mobile Troops also used this system to get their junior reserve officers. The new armoured and mechanised equipment necessitated special training and conversion courses for the reserve officers too.

These courses were held at Esztergomtábor at the Central Armoured and Motorised Rifle School.

NCO training

The professional NCOs were trained at the Kinizsi Pál NCN School at Veszprém/Juttas from 1924 until 1944. The NCO School had one-one infantry, artillery and mobile training battalion. The mobile battalion consisted of one-one cavalry

Commission pared held at Ludovica Academy in 1943. The Armoured Class vehicles can be seen in the foreground, Toldi, Turán and Nimrod armoured vehicles. [Mujzer Péter]

and armoured companies. From 1934, selected enlisted men could apply to the NCO School. The two years long training course was famously thought and demanding. The graduates were respected and feared by the conscripts and valued by the officers. The School had 4 Csaba armoured cars in 1944.

Enlisted training

Hungary was an agricultural nation with a relatively small industrial background. The cavalry training of the enlisted men was relatively easy due to the agricultural background of the

Field maintenance of a 39. M Csaba armoured car at the 1. Armoured Cavalry Battalion in 1941. [Móker József]

Mechanics surround a 38. M Toldi light tank. The tank has the late style military insignia and the white tulip unit sign of the 11. Cyclist-Tank Battalion which is contradict to each other. [Szollár János]

German conversion training was organised in Galicia for 3. Tank Regiment in summer of 1944. German and Hungarian officers were in charge of the conversion course. The Hungarian officer has a metal Tiger badge on his field cap. [Mariusz Zimny]

German Pz. V. tank introduced to Hungarian officers in 1944, Esztergomtábor. Next to the Panther, Hungarian armoured vehicles exhibited, 38. M Toldi, 40. M medium and 41. M heavy Turáns, Skoda 38(t) and 40. M Nimród. [Szollár János]

German 3,7cm Flak 43 auf Gw IV Mobelwagen AA vehicle also presented to the Hungarians at Esztergomtábor in 1944. [Szollár János]

country. However there were not enough well trained civilian drivers and mechanics that could operate the mechanised and armoured vehicles. The conscription was 2 years for every able bodied male citizen. Due to the war, the conscripts were not demobilised after two years or were recalled very frequently. The longer service time provided more opportunity to train the crew. Internal training program was created by the Army to train the men. Initially, due to the inexperienced

crews, there were a lot of technical failures during training and combat.

Most of the Polish trucks and tanks that had made their way to Hungary and had been interned after the occupation of Poland by Germany were used for training, and this equipment was largely written of during training by the inexperienced crews.

The "esprit de corps" of the Mobile Branch dated back to the old cavalry heritage of the Army, which was enlarged to cover the armoured, cyclist, motorised rifles as well as. They had worn the same sunflower blue branch colour on their uniforms. To be a member of the Mobile Branch was very popular among the officers, NCOs and men and it carried a high level of prestige.

German Influence

The largest training program undertaken outside of Hungary was the conversion of the 1st Armoured Field Division personnel in Germany in early 1942.

From 1941 to 1942 the training incorporated the lessons learned by German Army in its various campaigns, and German armoured tactics were adopted and adapted to the Hungarian situation. When the Armoured Divisions were organised these units had two and a half years to train the crews and prepare for combat. In the front lines the units were regularly trained by German "guest instructors" who gave lectures about the new methods, weapons. To prepare them for receiving German equipment, Hungarian crews were converted to use German techniques, with surprisingly fast and successful results. The Germans were surprised by the Hungarian skills and enthusiasm.

The Hungarian Mobile Troops were very brave but in the first phase of the war they were lack of the required skills and training of the modern warfare. The troops advanced without proper reconnaissance, fire and infantry support. They attacked the enemy positions frontally and suffered heavy casualties as a consequence. Often, contrary to tactical dictates, the tanks were deployed as stopgap or "infantry support" units. It has to be recognised that there were considerable technical differences between the T-34 and the Toldi tanks. This generated a fear of Russian techniques and an eagerness to receive better equipment.

Under normal circumstances, the success rate of the Hungarian armoured units was much the same as the enemy's, but where the Hungarians received more up-to-date equipment (Tiger, Panther and Zrínyi armoured vehicles) they had better results. Occasionally, during periods of retreat, abandoned (but serviceable) German tanks were picked up by the Hungarians and used against Soviet armour.

CHAPTER IV

European Armored Forces
Armored troops of the Middle-East European countries in 1938-1940

It is not useless to look at the strength and development of the armored / mobile troops of the surrounding Eastern European countries. The surrounding countries, with the exception of Austria, Bulgaria and Hungary, did not strike an unfair peace treaty that would have restricted the development of the armed force.

Before we look at on the armored / mechanized forces of each country, we must mention the theories that European countries modernized their army after the Great War. Based on the First World War experience, they sought to avoid a trench war with huge losses. As a means of rapid and decisive destruction of enemy forces, mobility / motorization and its counter measures (fortress lines) were considered.

During the First World War, maneuverability was represented by the corps of cavalry and air force.

In connection with the mechanization of the mainland forces in the 1920s and 1930s, four main trends evolved in Europe: English, French, German and Soviet.

Basically, each school tries to solve the problem of motorization by bridging the gap between cavalry corpses and mechanized forces. Of course, the degree and pace of mechanization was strongly influenced by the economic situation of the country and the level of development of its industry.

The theoretical views on the future war were also in connection with the military and political elite approach to the country's armed forces.

In 1928, the British Empire began to transform the cavalry regiments into a mechanized force, inspired by the industrial background and the decline in the stock of horses. From 1926 there was already an experimental armored unit.

France, based on the lessons learned from the Great War, began to organize armor cavalry units from 1928, beside the static fortress-based border protection. Mechanized cavalry divisions, Division Légere Mécanique were created.

Germany, from the beginning of the mid-20s, cooperating with the Soviet Union, worked on the development, theoretical and technical founding of an armored mechanized forces. The German supporters of armored-motorized warfare were thinking of creating a compact armored-mechanized force that worked in conjunction with the traditional infantry and horse drawn units that form the main bulk of the armed force.

The Soviet Union, based on the experiences of the civil war mobile operations, had a vision to deploy cavalry units and armored trains in an upcoming war. The new Soviet military doctrine, in line with political goals, prepared the army for large scale, deep offensive operations. The Red Army's order of battle, besides the traditional cavalry corpses consisted of mechanized and airborne corpses too.

Poland

Poland had the most significant armor force in the region. In 1939, the Polish Army had 3 light tank battalions, 11 armored reconnaissance battalions, 19 reconnaissance tankette companies, and 5 light tank companies.

The troops had 377 TK / TKS tankettes, 98 7TP, 45 R-35, 34 Vickers and 45 Renault FT-17 light tanks and 88 WZ. 29 and 34 armored vehicles, a total of 687 combat vehicles. The troops also had 10 armored trains.

Most of the armored units, however, were split between the infantry divisions and the cavalry brigades according to the French pattern. There were two mechanized brigades belonging to the Polish mechanized/armor branch.

The little antant countries, allies of France, took over the French military and organizational doctrines as well. The Czechoslovak, Yugoslav and Rumanian armies built serious border fortifications and followed the French example in the field of motorization. Of course, the proportion of horse-mechanized forces was heavily dependent on the country's industrial and financial potential

Czechoslovakia

Czechoslovakia, like one of the Little Entente states, had a serious military industrial background and it had one of the best equipped European armies in the 1930s. The Czech armed forces supported the mechanization and armored-motorized troops backed by a strong and modern military industry. Followed the French model, 4 mobile divisions (Division Légere Mécanique) were organized. Each mobile division consisted of one-one motorized and cavalry brigades battalion, one tank, one armored reconnaissance battalions, and division's artillery. A total of 114 combat vehicles consisted of the armored strength of the division. During the Czechoslovak crisis, the army had 298 LZ vz.35, 50 LT vz.34 light tanks, 70 vz.30 tankettes and 80 armored cars.

Slovakia

After the occupation and partition of Czechoslovakia, the Slovak Army had a much modest armor force during the Slovak-Hungarian border conflict of March 1939. Originally, the 3rd mobile division of the Czechoslovak Army was stationed in the Slovakian territory, but after the announcement of the new Slovak state, Czech nationality left the formation. In the summer of 1939, an armored battalion was organized for the remaining manpower and combat technique. The battalion consisted of an armored car, a light tank, an anti-tank, and a replacement companies. The troops had 27 LT vz.34, 52 LT vz.35 light tanks, 30 vz.30 tankettes and 20 vz.27, vz.30 armored cars.

In 1940, an armored regiment was organized, it consisting of a staff company, an armored battalion (1 armored car, 2 light tank companies), an anti-tank battalion (4 anti-tank companies) and a replacement battalion.

The Slovakian armored forces reported the slightest threat to the Hungarian army, though it was said of the entire Slovakian army.

Romania

The mechanization of the Romanian army and the organization and maintenance of armored troops were strongly hindered by the industrial underdevelopment of the country. Only foreign purchases could solve the development of armored forces. Interestingly the Romanian historians literally points to the development of the Hungarian military industry, the development and production of combat vehicles as a positive example to the Romanian.

In 1937, the Romanian Army ordered 35 CKDs (in the Romanian Army R-1) in order to equip the reconnaissance companies of the cavalry units. The 1. Tank Regiment was organized with 126 Skoda S-II (R-2) light tanks. The Romanian army gained a significant amount of Polish military equipment in 1939, when a significant part of the Polish army retreated to Romania.

The 2. Tank Regiment, set up in 1939, was equipped with 41 French and 34 Polish R-35 tanks.

The Rumanians have purchased the Renault UE light tracked armored tractor production right. The entire domestic production did not materialize, the engine of the tractor was transported from France. Until 1941, only 126 vehicles were made. Later the Germans handed over to the Romanians more UE tractors from the war booty material, and about 178 pieces were handed over to the troops.

By the end of the 30s, the Romanian Army mechanized 3 cavalry and 2 rifle regiments, as well as two tank regiments. The units had 236 light tanks and 178 armored tracked tractors. In 1940, this amount of armor overcame the combat vehicles of the Hungarian Army in both numbers and qualities.

Yugoslavia

The Yugoslav Army did not have a significant armor force. Although in 1921 they had a tank battalion with 50 FT-17 armored vehicles. In 1940 two tank battalions were in the battle order. In addition to the obsolete FT-17, there were 24 R-35 tanks.

Austria

Like Hungary, Austria was under the strict military provisions of the peace treaty ending the First World War. The more developed Austrian industry, however, provided more room for maneuver in the army's motorization. The Austrian military industry produced various armored vehicles (ADGZ, ADKZ), wheeled-tracked vehicles (ADMK Mulus) and wheeled-tracked armored artillery tractors (Saurer RK-7). Like Hungary, the Austrians also bought 72 CV 35 Italian tankettes. Of the ADGZ heavy armored car, 12 served at the Army and 15 served in the police. The rapid division was set up in 1935, with a 1-1 cavalry and motorized brigade, 1 armored battalion (1 armored car and 2 tankette companies), a motorized artillery regiment, 1 mechanized signal battalion and 1 mechanized sapper company.

Bulgaria

The development of the Bulgarian Army was hampered not only by the provisions of the peace treaty, but by the backward industrial and economic situation of the country. The first fighting vehicle was procured in 1934, 14 pcs of CV 35 tankettes. The Bulgarian bought 8 Vickers light tanks in 1938. In 1939, a tank battalion was created from the existing two armored companies. In 1940, 36 Skoda LT-35 light tanks were taken from the Germans. Next year, 40 French R-35 light tanks also arrived from Germany. The LT-35 and R-35 fighting vehicles were organized into two tank battalions. In 1941, the two battalions were put together in a tank regiment.

Hungary

By comparing these numbers and figures with the armored forces of the Hungarian Army in 1939, only 151 35. M FIAT Ansaldo tankettes served at the 2 cavalry and 2 motorized rifle brigades' reconnaissance and armored cavalry battalions. The 38. M Toldi light tanks and 39. M Csaba armored cars were only handed over to the troops in the summer of 1940. By September 1940, only 50 light tanks delivered to the troops. Just 54 combat and 8 training (iron) Csaba armored cars were serviceable in 1940.

The Axis Armoured troops in the second part of the WWII

The Axis Forces were deeply committed in the war against the Soviet Union and elsewhere fighting with the Allied Powers. The pre-war developments and theories of the armoured-mechanised warfare, the organisation and the equipment of the armoured forces were overwritten by the escalation of the war, especially on the Eastern Front, where the minor axis forces faced with the formidable, rebirth Soviet Armed Forces.

Romanian armoured forces

The most significant contribution was provided by the Romanian Armed Forces to support the German Forces on the Eastern Front.

The 1st Romanian Panzer Division, later known as "Romania Mare", ("Great Romania"), was built from different motorized components of the Romanian army in April, 1941, baptised in fire during the Barbarossa Campaign. It was equipped with 126 R-2 and 75 R-35 light tanks and 28 armoured cars. The division was refitted and deployed again for the Stalingrad Campaign in 1942. The Germany provided a number of Panzer III medium tanks, Panzer IV medium tanks and Pz. 38t light tanks as well as armoured cars, half-tracks and antitank guns. The armoured element consisted of 100 R-2 light tanks, 10-10 Pz. III and Pz.IV medium tanks and 28 SdKfz. 222 armoured cars and 14 SdKfz. 251 half-tracks.

Most of this combat equipment was lost in the winter of 1942/1943. The 1st Romanian Panzer Division then had to wait for replacement equipment to be delivered from Germany and did not see action for more than a year; it never fought as a division again.

Finish armoured forces

The Finnish Supreme headquarters ordered the foundation of an armoured division on 28 June 1942. The division consisted of the newly formed Armoured Brigade and the Jaeger Brigade. The Cavalry Brigade was also part of the division until January 1943. The armoured brigade has two tank battalions, mostly equipped with captured ex-Soviet T-26 light tanks and few T-34 medium tanks. The division also had one assault gun battalion with 30 StuG III and one self-propelled AA battery with 6 Ladswerk vehicles. The Jager Brigade had 3 jager battalions. The division also had one-one anti-tank, heavy artillery, signal and engineer battalions.

Italian armoured forces

At the beginning of the war, the armoured divisions were filled with L3 tankettes. Initially, a total of about 100 M11 tanks were also available. An armoured division included one tank regiment, one artillery regiment, one Bersaglieri (light infantry) regiment, divisional supply units and a mixed engineer company. The tank regiment could have between three and five tank battalions. At full strength, each battalion had 55 tanks.

Later on sufficient numbers of the M13/40 tanks and its upgrades were available. The Italians also developed several self-propelled 75 mm guns on the M13 platform. While always in short supply, 57 of the 90 mm guns were ordered to be mounted on heavy trucks (Autocannoni da 90/53) to enhance mobility. 48 guns were mounted on a M14/41 tank chassis as Tank Destroyer 90/53 (Semovente 90/53).

Tab. 1. Comparative strength of the Hungarian and minor Axis armoured divisions

	Hungarian AD 1942	Romanian AD 1944	Finnish AD 1943	Italian AD 1943	Bulgarian AD 1942
Strenght	13000 men	11,870 men	7000 men	7500 men	**9,340 men**
Medium tanks	114 xTurán 40M	90 × R-4 (PzIV) medium tanks	18 x T-34,	48 xM15/42	90xPz.VI.
Heavy tanks	66x Turán 41M		2 x KV-1		
Light tanks	87x Toldi 38M	21 Pz. II	87 x T-26		16x Pz.35(t) 16x Pz.38(t)
Armoured cars	13xCsaba 39M	30 × SdKfz. 222 armored cars 20 × SdKfz. 251 half-tracks		50	18x SdKfz. 222, 223
AA vehicles	42x Nimród 40M		6x Landswerk		
SP AT guns		10 × TACAM T-60 (7.62cm guns)	18 x BT-42	15 x Semovente 47mm	
SP guns		22 × TA (StuG III—7.5cm guns)	30x StuGIII	132 x 75mm 12x 105mm Semovente	
Artilerry	24x light howitzer	12 × 10.5 FH18 12 × Skoda M19 10cm howitzers 28 × 7.5cm Reisita	12x 15cm heavy howitzers	24x 7,5cm guns	8 x heavy field howitzers 12 x light field howitzers
AA artillery	9 x Bofors	12 × 2.5 cm, 12 × 2cm		16x2cm	27
AT guns	22	6 × 5cm PAK 38 11 × 4.7cm	12		36
Mortars	12	6 × 12cm, 14 × 8.1cm	8x8,1cm		40
Light mortars	20	27 × 6cm			
AT rifles	26				
Machine guns	36	749 light,heavy	52		192
Light machine guns	144				378

Tab. 2. Comparative strength of the Hungarian and major forces armoured divisions

	Hungarian AD 1942	German AD 1943	Soviet AC 1943	British AD 1944	US AD 1942
Strenght	13000 men	13700 men	7853 men	14964 men	10973 men
Medium tanks	114 Turán 40M	91 Pz. III	98 T-34	246	232
Heavy tanks	66 Turán 41M	34 Pz. IV			
Light tanks	87 Toldi 38M	21 Pz. II	70 T-70	63	158
Armoured cars	14 Csaba 39M			87	79
AA vehicles	42 Nimród 40M	57		45	
SP AT guns		31		24	126
SP guns		12		24	96
Artilerry	24 light howitzer	24 howitzer	27 field guns	24	
AA artillery	9 Bofors	20	2	380	
AT guns	22	12	12	54	
Mortars	12	18	52	28	27
Light mortars	20	30		132	57
AT rifles	26				
Machine guns	36	263		22	103
Light machine guns	144			1300	290
Rocket launchers			8		

In 1943, the Ariette Armoured Cavalry Division was made up of one armoured reconnaissance group, one-one armoured cavalry, motorised infantry, self-propelled artillery, motorised artillery regiments and one anti-tank battalion

Bulgarian armoured forces

Bulgarian Armoured Brigade order of battle consisted of one-one tank, motorised infantry, artillery regiments and one-one armoured reconnaissance, anti-tank, AA and engineer battalions in July 1944. The Bulgarian armoured forces were deployed against their former allies in 1944-1945.

The table 1 is about the comparative strength of the minor axis power in the second half of the war. We must recognise that the official order of battles rarely met with the reality due to the shortages of equipment, battle loses.

Table 2 shows the comparative strength and the firepower of the Hungarian and the main belligerent powers' armoured divisions. It is also applicable that the theoretical and the real strength of the division varied due to the shortages and battle loses.

CHAPTER V

Brief operational history of the Hungarian armoured forces
Peacetime Operations

First Vienna Arbitrage

In 1938, during the Czechoslovakian Crisis the Hungarian governments carried out unsuccessful negotiations concerning the Hungary's territorial requests. The forces of both countries were placed on a state of alert.

The seven tankette companies of the Hungarian Army were formed and equipped with crews and material ready for combat, should the need have arisen. The companies created their own unit insignia and waited for deployment.

Following the Vienna Arbitrage, Hungarian troops peacefully occupied Upper-Hungary from 5 to 10 of November 1938. Four infantry corps (former mixed brigades), the I, II, VI, VII, took part in this mission with their tankette and cavalry companies, and cyclist battalions. The armoured trains also were deployed as forward units of the advancing troops.

Occupation of Trans-Carpathian Ukraine

After the total occupation of the Czech state by Germany and the establishment of a Slovakian puppet state, Hungarian forces began to occupy the disputed territory on March 15. The 2nd Motorised Infantry and the 2nd Cavalry Brigades' cavalry, cyclist and motorised infantry battalions, Ansaldo tankette companies and troops of the VI and VII Corps advanced and reached the Polish border on March 17.

The advance was not peaceful. The tankette companies involved in the fighting on 17. and 23. of March.

During the operation many of the Ansaldos broke down due to mechanical failure. The tankettes lacked spare parts, tracks and transport vehicles.

Operation Transylvania

For Hungary the loss of Transylvania, because of its size, population and resources, was the biggest blow resulting from the Trianon Treaty, which had awarded this territory to Romania.

To back up their demands, the Hungarians mobilised their armed forces; as of July 10, three armies were deployed in the south-east part of Hungary. The mobile troops were allocated a vital role in the planned operations against the Romanian forces. After breaking through the Romanian defences of the Carol Line, the Mobile Corps was to pursue and destroy the withdrawing enemy. The Mobile Corps was formed with two cavalry and two motorised rifle brigades; however these units were incomplete as regards military hardware. The armoured and reconnaissance battalions had received most of their 38. M Toldi light tanks and 39. M Csaba armoured cars at the assembly area only at the last minute. The factory-fresh vehicles were incomplete and had a lot of mechanical failures.

The armoured troops were at 2/3 strength, and only forty 38. M Toldi tank were with the light tank companies. The four armoured car companies had only 11 combat and 2 training (iron) 39. M Csaba at that time. On August 27, one third of the 35. M Ansaldos were still under repair, the spare tracks would not arrive until October. The motorised infantry battalions got the new 38. M Botond trucks, which also arrived at the assembly area.

The military occupation of Northern Transylvania was carried out from 5 to 13 of September. The poor state of the roads created many mechanical problems for the mobile forces. The majority of the tanks fresh from the factory and the mobilised civilian trucks broke down and had to be withdrawn from service without even having seen any enemy activity. This

35. M Ansaldo tankettes belong to the 1. Reconnaissance Battalion, 1. Motorised Rifle Brigade. The huge white unit sign, lightning bolt painted on the side of the vehicles in 1938. [Bonhardt Attila]

35. M Ansaldo tankette platoon parked in an occupied Carpathian-Ukrainian tow Munkács, in 1939, the house behind the tankettes sprayed with bullets. The occupation was a low intensity operation. [Bonhardt Attila]

The Hungarian troops captured two Slovakian Lt. vz. 35 light tanks during the Trans-Carpathian operation, later incorporated to the Hungarian Armoured forces for evaluation and training. [Fortepan 107680]

mobilisation and occupation highlighted many problems for the armoured and mobile troops. The lessons were identified as follows: lack of well-trained crews, lack of personnel with maintenance background, lack of spare parts, poor equipment (Ansaldo tankettes), and questionable command skills. On the plus side the Northern Transylvania action also showed the high spirit of the troops.

The troops had received the new 38. M Toldi and 39. M Csaba vehicles, and 38. M Botond trucks in a piecemeal fashion. At the end of the mission the armoured and wheeled vehicles had to be sent for maintenance to military and civilian repair shops.

Yugoslavian Campaign

On April 6, 1941 the German Army attacked Yugoslavia. Hungary was one of the assembly points for the German troops. Soon after the beginning of the German attack, an independent Croatia was declared, and the Hungarian 3rd Army (I, IV, V Corps) and the Mobile Corps, with supporting troops, began their attack on April 11.

The Mobile Corps was comprised of the 1st and 2nd Cavalry and the 1st and 2nd Motorised Infantry Brigades. The mobile troops were in the midst of reorganising the new tank bat-

In September 1939 the withdrawing Polish units arrived to Hungary, Polish TK tankett transported by truck belonged to the 10. Armoured Cavalry Brigade. [Fortepan 78266]

Assembled TK/TKS tankettes of the reconnaissance company of the 10. Armoured Cavalry Brigade in Hungarian territory, late September 1939. [Fortepan 78270]

talions. The armoured cavalry battalions received their two tankette companies, but without the 38. M Toldi platoons. Due to the slowness of mobilisation and a lack of armaments, the forces were not at full strength.

When the Hungarian forces began their attack, the Serb fortifications were partially abandoned by the regular Serb troops. The Hungarian forces occupied this territory after only minor clashes.

As of April 14, the motorised brigades of the Mobile Corps were reassigned to the German Panzer Group Kleist, however the campaign came to a swift conclusion and they were assigned the duty of securing the area of Eszék (Osijek) –Vinkovci –Vukovár (Vukovar). During the campaign two of the five officers killed belonged to the armoured forces, serving with the armoured car troops. Two 39. M Csaba armoured cars was knocked out and several armoured vehicles were damaged by mines.

Soviet Campaign 1941

On June 26, 1941 three unidentified twin-engine bombers attacked the Hungarian town of Kassa (Kosice). The following morning Hungarian bombers attacked Russian targets in Ukraine, and Russia and Hungary were at war.

An operational group was formed to carry out the military activity against Russia. It was called the "Carpathian Group", commanded by Lt. Gen. Ferenc Szombathelyi, and consisted of the VIII Corps (1st Mountain Brigade and 8th Frontier Guard Brigade) and the Mobile Corps. The Mobile Corps was led by Maj. Gen Béla dálnoki Miklós and comprised of three brigades: the 1st and 2nd Motorised Rifle and 1st Cavalry Brigades. The Mobile Corps was reinforced with the I, V, VIII Artillery Battalions, the VI, VII Cyclist Battalions, and the 152nd Engineer and 150th Signal Battalions.

Under the new organisation, the motorised rifle brigades had one light tank battalion and one reconnaissance battalion, and

Polish 40mm Bofors AA gun battery and half-tracked artillery tractors resting in Hungarian territory, September 1939. [Fortepan 78278]

38. M Botond squad carrier truck decorated with flowers but armed with 31. M squad automatic weapon during the operation in Transylvania. [Fortepan 15601, Erky-Nagy Tibor]

The artillery battalions of the Mobile Corps during the occupation of Transylvania, were equipped with 37. M Hansa Lloyd half tracked artillery tractors and 37. M 10,5cm light howitzers. The unit sign, white pennant painted on the gun shield as well as on the back of the vehicles. [Mujzer Péter]

38. M Toldi light tanks belong to the 1. Reconnaissance Battalion enter into a small Transylvanian village in September 1940. The 1. Reconnaissance Battalion invented its own military sign, Maltese cross, painted on the armoured vehicles. [Szollár János]

the cavalry brigade had one armoured battalion. The 1st Motorised Rifle Brigade had the 9th Cyclist-Tank Battalion, and the 2nd Brigade had the 11th Cyclist-Tank Battalion. The battalions' title and organisation reflected on the transitional sate of them.

The armoured elements of the Mobile Corps had 81-87 Toldi light tanks, 48 Csaba armoured cars and 60 Ansaldo tankettes.

The "Carpathian Group" began its advance on June 30, through very difficult mountainous terrain. The withdrawing

Rest and maintenance carry out at the Tankette Company of the 1. Reconnaissance Battalion in Transylvania. The Ansaldos tankettes wear the white skulls and lightning bolt insignia plus the large Maltese cross military insignia. [Szollár János]

38. M Toldi light tank, number plate H-344 waits at Transylvania 1940. The tank belongs to the Light Tank Company of the 1. Armoured Cavalry Battalion. The white arching horseman was the early unit sign of the Light Tank Company. [Szollár János]

Advancing 39. M Csaba armoured car belongs to the 1. Reconnaissance Battalion followed by local Hungarian civilians in Voivodina, April 1941. [Szollár János]

Red Army created obstacles for the advancing Hungarian troops by blowing up bridges wherever it could.

The task of the Hungarian forces was to maintain the connection between the 17th German Army and the 3rd Romanian and 11th German Armies, and to stop the withdrawing Red Army units.

From July 9, the Mobile Corps was subordinated to the German Army Group South, to support the 17th German Army, while the VIII. Corps remained in the rear areas to act as a security force.

The troops lacked of recovery vehicles and trailers. The maintenance background of the troops was also weak, and the mobilised civilian trucks were in bad condition. Only the 38M Botond trucks could handle the difficult terrain.

The armoured vehicles were sometimes deployed incorrectly, contrary to normal procedures, which caused greater casualties than otherwise may have been incurred. The commanding officers were in real war in first time with equipment and rules of engagement never tested before. They were not aware of the real advantages or disadvantages of the armoured and mobile units and their equipment's. Sometimes the commanders issued orders which led to suicide actions.

Due to the large number of mechanical problems, civilian technician groups were organised and sent to the front from the Manfred Weiss, Ganz, and MAVAG factories on July 18. A separate group was organised to deal with the 30 mechanically broken-down Ansaldos.

The 1st and 2nd Motorised and the 1st Cavalry Brigades continued their attack against Nikolayev from 16 to 17 August.

The mobile troops were allowed a brief period of rest between August 17-27, to recuperate following the long advance.

The Armoured Car Company of the 1. Reconnaissance Battalion waits for the road opening. Interestingly the first Csaba armoured car decorated with garlands, this operation was not really about the celebration in 1941. [Szollár János]

Csaba armoured car platoon and Ford trucks wait in the assemble area for the marching order in June 1941 at the Hungarian-Soviet border. Interesting that the camouflage pattern of the armoured cars and canvas protective covers are identical. [Szollár János]

38. M Toldi tank, belongs to the 2. Reconnaissance Battalion, is on the way to Voivodina 1941. In the background a Ford-Marmon truck is visible. [Fortepan 71498, Lissák Tivadar]

Mechanised artillery battalion prepares to move to the assembly area to support the operation against Russia. The 37. M light howitzers towed by 37. M Hansa Lloyd tractors. The 38. M Botond trucks mainly belong to the motorised rifle battalions. [Mujzer Péter]

Hungarian soldiers examine a 38. M Toldi light tank, number plate H-332 run over a mine. The weapons removed from the turret, the tank still has the old 1. Reconnaissance Battalion sign in July of 1941. [Szollár János]

Burned out 39. M Csaba armoured car, number plate Pc.125 belongs to the 1. Reconnaissance Battalion at Rogazna in July 1941. [Szollár János]

On September 1, the Corps was reassigned to defend the River Dnieper, south of Dnepropetrovsk.

From 27 September to 11 October, the Mobile Corps received a respite from the fighting in order to reorganise and recover, in an area south of Tomakovka.

The Hungarian forces reached the River Donets at Isium -South on October 28-29.

The Mobile Corps ceased combat on November 6 and returned to Hungary. During the four months of operations, the Corps covered 2000 kilometres. The overall causalities came to 10% of the men and 100% of the 35. M Ansaldo, 90% of the 39. M Csaba armoured car and 80 % of the 38. M Toldis. Out of 95 38. M Toldi tanks, 62 were sent to the factory for repair, while 25 were destroyed. 1200 trucks and 28 guns were also lost during the campaign. In terms of manpower, 855 men were killed, 2845 wounded or missing, and 830 were unavailable due to illness.

Due to the lessons learned from the campaign, the 35. M Ansaldo was removed from service, as it had become clear that

Hungarian dispatch rider passes a knocked out Soviet Ba-10 armoured cars on the highway in Russia 1941. He wears light uniform without any protective gear probably far away from the heat of the battle. [Fortepan 27465, Mészöly Leonóra]

Krupp Protze truck belonges to the 4. Motorised Rifle Battalion heavy weapon company, the 07/31. M Schwarzlose machine gun on AA mount during the Russian Campaign in 1941. [Mujzer Péter]

Resting crew sit on a 38. M Toldi light tank in Russia 1941. The armoured vehicle carries the unit sign of the 1. Cavalry but probably belongs to 9. Cyclist-Tank Battalion. [Szollár János]

Crew of the 38. M Toldi light tank take a rest during the fight, some of them wear mechanics overalls. In the background a Ford Marmon truck is visible. [Szollár János]

Abandoned BT-7A artillery tank with short barrel 7,6cm howitzer surrounded by Hungarian officers and locals in a Ukrainian town in 1941. [Szollár János]

Hungarian Armored Forces in World War II

38. M Toldi tank tows a broken down Italian truck. Next to the tank is a 38. M Botond truck, by that time the only wheeled vehicle which was able to negotiate the muddy terrain. [Szollár János]

After the operation of the Mobile Corps, the armoured and non-armoured vehicles needed a full, factory level maintenance, carried out at the factories and at the workshop of the Automobile Depot. On the picture are 38. M Toldi light tanks and an 35. M Ansaldo tankett in 1942. [Fortepan 72518, Lissák Tivadar]

light tanks could not perform the duties of medium or heavy tanks. The troops begged for new and better equipment, but it was not a question of lack of willingness, rather the limitations were set by the capacity of the war industry to meet the demand.

Armoured units in Russia 1942-1943

In 1942 the Germans had changed their mind about the role of the Hungarian forces in the war. The Hungarians offered Germany's Chief of the High Command, Field Marshal Keitel, a complete field army, the 2nd Army.

The 2nd Hungarian Army had three infantry corps with nine light divisions (each with two infantry and one artillery regi-

ment) and one armoured division and a regiment-sized aviation group, plus supporting units, a total of 250,000 men. However, the Hungarians had no armoured equipment available for the armoured division, so the material needed to equip it was purchased from Germany. The division was designated the 1st Armoured Field Division. It was an ad hoc unit, organised from different active mobile units which provided the manpower and equipment except the tanks.

The Germans provided Pz.Kpfw. IV and Skoda 38(t) tanks for the division, and organised special training for the crews.

The armoured equipment comprised of 24 Pz. IVF-1, 108 Skoda 38(t), 14 x 39M Csaba, 18 x 38M Toldi and 19 x 40M Nimród armoured vehicles plus 6 Pz. Befehlwagen command vehicles .

The Hungarians received German equipment to mobilise the 1. Armoured Field Division. The Hungarians got a few SdKfz 251 half-tracked armoured medical vehicles. The Pc-021 parks alongside other vehicles at the Automobile Depot in 1942. [Fortepan 72259, Lissák Tivadar]

Skoda 38(t) tank, turret number 523, and its crew belong to the 2. Platoon, 5. Company of the 30/II Tank Battalion, at Esztergomtábor, before the deployment to Russia in 1942. [Markó Ferenc]

The units of the Division were transported by rail to Russia and after the disembarkation the troops reached the operations area from 2 to 6 of July.

The Hungarian 2nd Army was assigned to support the left wing of the German advance to destroy the Red Army at Stalingrad. It was subordinated to the German Army Group B together with the 6th German and 8th Italian Armies.

The main goal of the Hungarian forces was to overcome the Red Army units and reach the River Don in order to establish a de-

Abandoned Russian KV-1 tank used for testing the armoured piercing capability of the light anti-tank guns of the Hungarian Army at the river Don. This armoured-piercing shell logged into the thick armour without any effect. [Fortepan 43106, Konok Tamás id.]

Battalion staff of the 30/II Tank Battalion crosses a creek. The Skoda 38(t) tank follows by a 38. M Toldi medical tank. One medical Toldi was subordinated to each tank battalions. The wheeled vehicles cross the bridge. [Móker József]

Skoda 38(t) tank company returns in a victorious mood after the first bridge head battle of Uryv in 22 of July 1942. [Mujzer Péter]

During the battle of Ury the Hungarians captured two "lend-lease" M3A1 Stuart light tank. Later on the Stuarts were used as towing vehicles for the Division. [Fortepan 14317, Csontos Péter]

Advancing Pz. IVF-1 tanks were the only armoured vehicles to match the Red Army medium tanks. These tanks belong to the heavy companies of the tank battalions. [Mujzer Péter]

Watching the air activity, 38(t) belongs to the Staff Company of the 30/II Tank battalion in August of 1942. [Móker József]

Due to the intensive air activity of the Red Air Force the precious armoured vehicles were heavily camouflaged. A 38(t) tank belongs to the 30/I Tank Battalion rests next to a building. [Mujzer Péter]

fence line along the river. The Hungarians had to hold a line that exceeded 200 kilometres in length, even though they did not have enough forces or equipment to perform their allowed task properly.

The 2nd Army units advanced and reached the River Don, but several Soviet bridgeheads of varying sizes remained on the Hungarian side of the river, posing a danger to the Hungarian defence. The commander of the 2nd Army, Colonel-General Gusztáv Jány, decided to mop up these bridgeheads with the support of the armoured division.

The 1st Armoured Field Division took part in the heaviest fighting of the bridgehead operations during the summer of 1942 at the River Don. It suffered heavy casualties partly due to the stubborn enemy resistance and partly because it was not deployed as an armoured division. Its individual units were used separately as close support mobile artillery, because the Hungarians lacked the necessary assault gun units to support the infantry.

Out of the three major Russian bridgeheads, the one at Korotoyak destroyed, on September 3.

To compensate the technical losses the Germans handed over 10 Pz. IVF-2, 10 Pz.III-M and probably 4-8 Pz. II-F tanks to the Hungarians in October 1942. Another 10 Stug III-N with German crew was subordinated in December.

The Armoured Division was withdrawn from the front line and placed in reserve. The units of the Armoured Division were withdraw from the front line and started to prepare the winter accommodation for the troops and equipment.

The 1st Armoured Field Division was subordinated to Group Cramer, which constituted the only reserve of Amy Group B, on January 2, 1943.

The Red Army broke through the Hungarian defences at 12-14 of January. After bitter fighting, the Russian forces enveloped and destroyed the outnumbered Hungarian units.

The Armoured Division was directly subordinated to the Germans and without their permission it was not allowed to be used for counter-attacks. The 1st Armoured Field Division was finally deployed on January 16 at Volcsej, to seal the gaps, but it was too late and its strength was too weak. The cold

The German 611. Panzerjäger Abteilung supported the Hungarian units at Ury in September 1942. Hungarian junior officers and the German crew pose with a Marder tank hunter vehicle. [Szollár János]

The autumn rain made difficult the movement for trucks. A Polski-Fiat 508 light truck according to its unit sign belongs to a maintenance unit stuck in the mud in 1942. [Fortepan 43121, Konok Tamás id.]

After the bridgehead battles the 1. Armoured Field Division was withdraw as a reserve unit. The vehicles were put into permanent winter shelters. On the picture the 38(t) tanks belonged to the 2. Company, 30/I Tank Battalion, parked under winter shelter. [Mujzer Péter]

The strength of the 1. Armoured Field Division was augmented by 9 Pz. III operated by German crew in January 1943. German, Hungarian soldiers and a Russian hiwi/volunteer pose on the picture. [Szollár János]

The 1. Armoured field Division was just deployed in mid-January to counter the Red Army offensive. A 38(t) tank in winter camouflage waits for order in January 1943. [Móker József]

Due to the extreme low temperature the crew frequently could not start the engines. The armament of the 38(t) tanks are in a protective canvas cover. [Móker József]

The really effective AA defence started with 40mm Bofors gun's armed 40. M Nimród Sp.AT/AA vehicle. The Nimród belongs to the 15. Bycicle Battalion, '. Cavalry Division. The divisional sign can be seen on the front hull of the vehicle, white horse shoe with dot. [Szollár János]

38. M Toldi light tank belonged to the 102. Occupational Armoured Company in Ukraine, the trooper armed with MP 40 sub-machine gun. [Karai Sándor]

38. M Toldi light tank belonged to the 2. Armoured Division in dark olive green camouflage towing a 38. M Botond signal truck. [Karai Sándor]

39. M Csaba armoured car with factory fresh dark olive green camouflage [Fortepan 72480, Lissák Tivadar]

40. M Nimród Sp. AT/AA vehicles with three tone camouflage mainly used for air defence and support role, the thin armour and inadequate gun made it unsuitable as a tank hunter. [Mujzer Péter]

weather and the deep snow also created major obstacles for the Hungarian operations. The division's task was to support and cover the withdrawing Hungarian forces, and to occupy and secure Nikolayevka and Alekseyevka, which lay along the route of escape.

The 1st Armoured Field Division suffered heavy casualties during the winter battles, losing almost all its armour due to

Abandoned 40. M Turán medium tank in Galicia, after the battles ended, the main armaments removed by the Soviet troops. [Szollár János]

Knocked out 40. M Turán medium tank in April 1944, Galicia, the tank blown due to direct hits into its turret. [Mujzer Péter]

Captured 40. M Turán medium tank prepared for towing by Soviet troops in summer of 1944 Galicia. [Mujzer Péte]

the deep snow, lack of fuel and enemy action. The division had only around 8000 men, 500 vehicles and 13 guns in March 1943. About ten armoured vehicles survived the battles. Nine Skoda 38(t), one Pz.IV and two Marders armoured vehicles were transported back to Hungary. The Marders were later returned to Germany.

Armoured Troops with the Occupation Forces in the Ukraine, 1941-44

The Hungarian Occupation Forces were reinforced with some captured French armoured vehicles in 1942. The 101st, 102nd and

40/43. M Zrínyi assault howitzers of the 3. Battery, 1. Assault Gun Battalion assembling for advance in Galicia 1944.[Szollár János]

probably a third, the 103rd Occupation Armoured Companies were raised between 1942-44.

The 101st Independent Tank Company consisted of one heavy and three light platoons. The heavy platoon had two SOMUA S-35, the light platoons had 15 Hotchkiss H-35 tanks handed over by the Germans. The tanks of the 101st Company were deployed all around the area of operation of the Occupation Forces. They were involved in convoy escort, road clearing, guerrilla hunting, and penalty strikes. The tanks were transported on rail, attached to improvised armoured trains as mobile support vehicles. The French armoured vehicles were lost or destroyed by their crew during the operation against partisans and regular Russian forces.

The 102nd Independent Armoured was organised by the 1/II Tank Battalion in 1943. The Company had two light tank platoon with 3-3 Toldi tank and two armoured car platoon with 3-3 Csaba armoured car. The task of the Company was to provide a mobile reserve for the Occupation Force East. The unit was deployed in December 1943 to Kremenyec, later moved to Stanislau.

The 102nd Company was disbanded upon the arrival of the 2nd Armoured Division to Galicia in April of 1944.

In 1943 the VII Cyclist Battalion was also deployed within the Occupation Forces, with two cyclist companies, and one armoured car and one support company. The armoured car company had 8 Csaba armoured cars.

The Hungarians also operated two former Polish and Soviet armoured trains to protect the rail lines.

The 2nd Armoured Division in Galicia, 1944

Face with the rapid advance of the Russian forces, the 1st Hungarian Army was mobilised and deployed in the Carpathian Mountains in the spring of 1944. However, the Germans ordered the Hungarians to move the 1st Army out of the well-constructed defence lines of the Carpathian Mountains and into Galicia. The task of the Hungarian forces was to advance and stabilise the situation between the German Army Groups North-Ukraine and South-Ukraine along the line of Kolomea-Ottyina-Stanislavov.

40. M Turán medium tank with reserve officers, the junior officers, troop, platoon leaders were normally reserve officers. [Szollár János]

The 1st Army comprised of 3 light infantry (2 regiments each), 3 infantry divisions (with 3 infantry regiments each), two mountain brigades and the 2nd Armoured Division.

The 2nd Armoured Division was mobilised on March 13 and was the most powerful unit of the 1st Army. The division was equipped totally with Hungarian produced armour: 40. M, 41. M

Well camouflaged Souma S35 tank belongs to the 101. Occupational Armored Company in 1943, covers the entrance of a Polish village. [Szollár János]

The 1. Tank Cavalry Battalion was equipped with medium and heavy Turán tanks, maintenance of the 40. M Turán tanks at the vehicle depot of an Army barrack. [Szollár János]

When Romania left the Axis side, the Hungarian-Romanian border was patrolled by a makeshift Hungarian armoured train. It consisted of flatcars and a 40. M Turán tank. The tank was immobile due to the engine failure but the armament worked. [Szollár János]

Another shot on the armoured train. Some of the crew armed with small arms, 31. M light machine gun and rifle, takes position on the tank turret. [Szollár János]

Reserve Ensigns sit on a 39. M Csaba armoured car. They took part in conversion training, summer of 1944. They were also drafted into the border screening troops in August of 1944. [Szollár János]

German and Hungarian troops gather around a PAK 40 anti-tank gun with RSO light tractor disembarked at a rail way station in Transylvania, 1944. [Szollár János]

Advancing 40/43. M Zrínyi assault howitzers belong to the 10. Assault Gun Battalion in the battle of Torda, 1944. The commanders leading the advance with open hatch. [Bonhardt Attila]

The Armoured Train no. 102. also fought in Transylvania, in autumn of 1944. The artillery wagon was armed with 8cm field gun in the turret.[Mujzer Péter]

The 36. M 40mm Bofors gun was a useful support to the mixed battle groups during the final battles. [Mujzer Péter]

Turán (medium and heavy), 40. M Nimród, 39. M Csaba and 38. M Toldi armoured vehicles. However, due to the slow rate of production, the armoured strength of the division was not at 100%.

It had 120 medium and 55 heavy Turáns, 84 light Toldi tanks and 42 Nimród A/A vehicles, as well as 14 Csaba armoured cars. Out of the 84 Toldis, 47 were armed with 40mm guns. The 3rd Tank Regiment was short of 18 medium and 14 heavy Turáns, one Toldi and two Nimród armoured vehicles. When the division was transported to the front, the Tank Regiment consisted of only two battalions, 3/I and 3/II. The third, (3/III Battalion) remained at home waiting for tanks. The 3/III Battalion joined the division at the front line only in July.

The units of the division, immediately upon arrival at the front line, were deployed separately to stabilise the front in a 60-70 km wide sector. The first task of the division was carried out in 17-19 of April. Nadvorna was captured and two bridgeheads were established on the River Bistrica. The Hungarian armoured units were supported by German tanks. According to the reports; 15 Marders, 5 Pz.IV and 8 Tiger tanks were added to the combat groups.

On April 17 the Turáns clashed first time with Russian tanks. The Hungarians knocked out two T-34 and lost of two Turán tanks north of Nadvorna. This was the baptism of fire for the Turán tanks against T-34 tanks.

The fight highlighted the disadvantages of the Turáns against the T-34. The T-34 could fire a deadly shot from 1500-2000 meters, while the heavy Turán needed 600 meters and the medium Turán 400 meters to destroy a T-34 in battle. The insufficient armoured protection was also painfully tested by the crew. The armour plates of the Turáns were not thick enough. Due to improper production the armour plate was fragile, in case of impact broken into pieces.

The 2nd Armoured Division captured Nadvorna and Delatyn at the end of April 18.

The second stage of the operation focused on the capture of the town of Kolomea. The terrain was very difficult; the thaw following winter had left the roads and fields muddy and the rivers flooded, creating obstacles for the advancing wheeled and tracked vehicles. The Red Army units used the terrain and the weather to their advantage and slowed down, then stopped the Hungarian advance on May 3, 1944, at Slobodka Lesna and Pocharnnyk.

The Division was withdrawn from the front line and became the reserve of the 1st Army on May 12. General Walter Model, commander of Army Group North-Ukraine, honoured the fighting skills of the Hungarian armoured forces. In May the division was partially re-equipped with German armour to compensate for its losses. The division received 12 Pz. IV

40. M Turán medium tank is ready to move, the commander wears 37. M crash helmet. The head lightsg are on the both side of the front hull.[Szollár János]

The 1. Armoured Division armoured vehicles were collected from different replacement and training units. This 41. M Turán heavy tank belongs to the Central Armoured and Motorised Rifle School at Esztergom. [Szollár János]

H, 10 Pz. VI E Tigers and 10 StuG III armoured vehicles at Nadvorna.

In July the Red Army launched an offensive against the Hungarian lines. The 2nd Armoured Division was put on alert and deployed at Stanislau on July 23. The Russian forces broke through at Ottyna, where the 3/I Tank Battalion could not stop them. The 1st Army was ordered to withdraw and the armoured troops were assigned to protect the troops as a rear guard.

The 1st Assault Gun Battalion, with the brand new 40/43. M Zrínyi assault howitzers were also assigned to the 1st Army. The 2nd and 3rd Batteries departed to the front on April 12, arriving on April 16.

The 7th Assault Gun Battalion was organised at Sümeg and replaced the 1st Battalion in the Carpathian Mountains in August 1944.

1st Cavalry Division on the Eastern Front

The 1st Cavalry Division was the pride of the Hungarian Army and the favourite of Regent Horthy. The division was reorganised and reinforced by armour and mechanised artillery units, and after the German occupation of Hungary, this unit was also slated for deployment on the front. The division was mobilised on April 29 1944.

The Hungarian General Staff wanted to deploy it as a subordinate unit of the 1st Army, however the Germans had another plan and the hussars were sent far from other Hungarian units, to the Pripet marshes. There they initially constituted the reserve of Lieutenant-General Walter Weiss' forces, the German 2nd Army, but within a short time they were thrown into the fray.

The division included the 1st Cavalry Tank Battalion with one heavy and three medium companies plus the staff company, altogether 25 x 38. M Toldis, 54 medium 40. M Turáns and 11 heavy 41. M Turán tanks. Other sources put the totals at 56 medium, 11 heavy Turáns and 5 light Toldi tanks, plus three 38(t) tanks for training. The hussars also had the 3rd Reconnaissance Battalion with two armoured car companies, each with 13 x 39. M Csaba armoured cars. The 15th Cyclist Battalion also had a company of four 40. M Nimród A/A-AT vehicles.

After the battle of Kletsk, until July 25, the Cavalry Division was in constant withdrawal in the direction of the River Vistula.

Further heavy fighting resulted in the division losing most of its vehicles and armaments.

An interesting episode to note concerning the Hussars occurred during the 1944 Polish uprising in Warsaw, when the Germans wanted to deploy the Cavalry Division against the Polish forces in the capital. Maj. Gen. Ibrányi refused to allow the division to participate directly in this action, informing the Germans that the long-standing tradition of Polish-Hungarian friendship precluded Hungarians from fighting Poles. The Cavalry Division's operations in Poland ended in late September 1944, and the division was transported back to Hungary.

2nd Armoured Division in Transylvania 1944

Following Romania's change of allegiance in September 1944, the Hungarian General Staff prepared a plan for the occupation of southern Transylvania. The intention was to form a defence line in the southern Carpathian Mountains and so prevent the Russians and their new Romanian allies from advancing into Hungarian territory.

The General Staff quickly organised and mobilised a new 2nd Army and reinforced it with the 2nd Armoured Division. On September 5 the Hungarians launched an offensive against overwhelmingly superior Romanian forces. The Hungarian forces comprised of three reserve infantry divisions, one light infantry division and one infantry division, two reserve mountain brigades, one frontier guard brigade and the 2nd Armoured Division. Facing them in Transylvania were the 1st and 4th Romanian Armies with 20 divisions.

The first stage of attack was successful and the Hungarian forces reached the town of Torda and crossed the Aranyos and Maros Rivers. However, the Russians increased the pace of their advance and successfully blocked the Hungarian drive towards the Carpathians. The Hungarian troops were forced to withdraw behind the river Maros and prepare for defence.

Taking part in the fighting were the 2nd Armoured Division, the 10th Assault Gun Battalion, and the 101st and 102nd armoured trains.

Due to the losses suffered in Galicia, the real strength of the division was depleted. According to the reports it had 14 x 38. M Toldis, 40 x 40. M medium Turáns, 14 x 41. M heavy Turáns, 21 x 40. M Nimróds and 12 x 39. M Csaba armoured vehicles. The Division was augmented with one Pz. III, nine Pz.IV-H, three Tiger H and one StuG. G armours. Around of 4 of September 20 Pz.IV H and five Panther tanks arrived to the units.

39. M Csaba armoured car, belongs to the 1. Reconnaissance Battalion. In the background a rocket launcher battery can be seen with WGr41 rocket launchers. The IV. Corps was reinforced with the 150. Rocket Launcher Battalion. [Mujzer Péter]

The Romanian defences collapsed in the face of the unexpected Hungarian attack.

The 2nd Armoured Division was placed in reserve on September 10, but was deployed again on September 13 at Torda. The Hungarians established a strong defence line around the town of Torda, which stopped the advancing Romanian-Russian forces between mid-September and mid-October. The 2nd Armoured Division was used as a mobile reserve and was deployed along critical points of the front line to carry out counter-attacks.

In early days of December 1944, the Division had 119 armoured vehicles, but only 17 operational. The Division had 26 x 40. M Nimrod, 8 x 39. M Csaba, 35 medium 40. M, 8 heavy 41.M Turán, 16 x 38. M Toldi, 1 Pz.III, 20 Pz.IV, 4 Panther and 1 StuG. III. By the end of this month 100 armoured vehicles was written off.

At the end of December 1944 and early days of January 1945, a smaller armoured battle group of the 2nd Armoured Division was subordinated to the Szent László Division which took part of the battle around river Garam. The Division, with 15 Pz. IV, three motorised rifle battalions and 3 batteries, took part in Operation Conrad I at Székesfehérvár from 7 to 12 January 1945. On January 7, 1945 the Soviet attacks of the 3rd German and 2nd Hungarian Armoured Divisions was halted at Csákvár.

1st Armoured Division in 1944/45

The Hungarian IV Corps was organised to block the advance of Russian-Romanian troops on the southern plains of Hungary at Arad and Lippa. The IV Corps was augmented with the VII Corps and later renamed as the 3rd Army also included the 1st Armoured Division. The troops assembled in the area of Makó – Nagyvárad, at 17 of September, 1944.

The 1st Armoured Division was only partially equipped at this time. The Division was removed from the Order of Battle, when its armament and equipment was handed over to the 2nd Armoured Division. However the 1st Armoured Division was mobilised again in August of 1944. The Division consisted of the 1st Tank Regiment with the 1/I and 1/III Battalions and 1st Motorised Rifle Regiment and one each of reconnaissance, A/A-AT, signal, and engineer battalions. The fire support based on an artillery regiment with one rocket-launcher and two artillery battalions. The reconnaissance battalion had one-one armour, motorcycle and motorised rifle company.

In the autumn of 1944 the 1st Tank Regiment lacked its tanks, so it was necessary to augment them from various training units. The 1st Assault Gun Battalion and the 2nd – 8th Assault Gun Training Cadres handed over 24 heavy Turán tanks to the 1st Tank Regiment. On September 2 the Division had only one tank battalion , the 1/III with a staff company (5 Toldis) and three medium companies (7 Turáns, 5 Toldis and 3 Nimróds/ company). The 1st Motorised Rifle Regiment had 9 Nimróds and the 51st A/A-AT Battalion had 18 Nimróds and three Toldi tanks. The divisional staff had two Nimróds. The 1st Reconnaissance Battalion had a mixed armoured car, light tank company where the Csaba armoured cars and Toldi light tanks of the Division were assembled.

The Division had 60-70 armoured vehicles before the start of the operation.

The Hungarian troop's main goal was to capture Arad, and advance along the Maros Valley up to the Zsil Valley to establish contact with the Hungarian 2nd Army. The Armoured Division was to attack the Romanian forces in successive waves from the area of Kevermes-Elek.

The 3rd Army commander requested the 1st Armoured Division to begin its offensive, to support the infantry and annihilate the Romanian troops. The Armoured Division surprised troops of the Romanian 1st Cavalry Division. The Hungarian Turáns attacked and destroyed a large Romanian cavalry group on the road at Macsa-Kürtös. The 1st Reconnaissance Battalion which was part of the second wave of the attack chased the withdrawing Romanian troops and occupied Arad.

The Corps level artillery consisted of hors drawn and mechanised artillery battalions, on the picture is a 31. M 15cm mechanised howitzers. [Mujzer Péter]

On September 16 the Hungarian tanks and infantry overran part of the Roman defence line, but the following day Russian armoured columns arrived and helped the Romanian forces to seal the gap. According to Romanian sources, 387 Hungarians were captured and 23 Toldi and Turán tanks knocked out compared to 377 Romanian casualties.

During the period up to October 11, the Hungarian armoured and anti-tank units knocked out 34 enemy tanks in the area of Szentes-Csongrád-Kecskemét.

On October 15, the Regent of Hungary, Admiral Horthy, attempted to declare an armistice with the Soviet Union as the prelude to Hungary leaving the Axis alliance and withdrawing from further involvement in the war. However, the Germans were alerted to the manoeuvre and instigated a pre-emptive take-over, assisted by supporters of the Hungarian "Arrow Cross" movement. The darkest chapter in Hungary's history during WWII had begun.

The Hungarian forces were subordinated to the Germans, and Hungary became a buffer zone between the Red Army and the Wehrmacht. On October 29, 1944 the 1st Armoured Division fought under the command of the German III Panzer Corps at Kecskemét.

Armoured trooper armed with hand grenade stands next to his 40. M Turán medium tank. The turret hatch is well visible on the picture. [Mujzer Péter]

This knocked out Pz. V Panther rest at Retek Street, Buda, not far from the current home of the author. [Fortepan 30884, Military Museum of Southern New England]

Assorted, knocked out armoured vehicles rest after the battle. Among the Soviet T-70 light tanks is an R-35. Most probably an ex- Polish vehicle used for training by Hungarians at Ludovika Academy. [Fortepan 32044, Ungváry Krisztián]

Siege of Budapest

Various elements of the 1st Armoured Division and 1st Hussar Division, and six assault gun battalions, as well as miscellaneous German and Hungarian units, were encircled in Budapest as of November 23, 1944.

At this time the 1st Armoured Division numbered 5000 men with three guns, seven tanks and three anti-tank guns and two battalions of infantry.

The six assault gun battalions, led by Lt. Gen. Ernő Bill-nitzer, commander of assault artillery troops, had 2000 men with 30 assault guns and 8 anti-tank guns. The battalions were equipped with Zrínyis and Hetzers, but as there were not a sufficient number of them, the majority of the trained crews were deployed as infantry. The assault guns provided a formidable threat to the advancing Russian troops. The size and armament of the Zrínyis were ideal for street fighting. Their low silhouette helped to conceal them, and the 10,5cm howitzer could penetrate any Russian armour at close range.

The siege of Budapest came to an end on February 13, 1945 when the Soviets overran the last of the defenders. The battle for the Hungarian capital had almost destroyed the city, and had caused many casualties among the civilian population. All of the Hungarian armour in the city was destroyed or captured during the fighting.

The Final Battles

Elements of Battle Group Horváth, led by Lt. Col Horváth, fought at Perbál with two Turáns, one Toldi and four Nimróds.

Battle Group Horváth's vehicles rest at the lake Velence in December 1944. On the picture one Botond truck, BMW R-75 motorcycles and one 40M Turán tank visible. [Szol-lár János]

Armoured Train nr. 103 painted with camouflage patches, in 1938. The armoured carriages equipped with observer and anti-tank rifle turrets. [Széplaki Gábor]

The armoured trains originated from WWI, the old fashioned hatches reflected on this fact. The so called flat artillery wagon was armed machine guns and 8cm field gun in the turret. [Szollár János]

Armed with 11 tanks and the remnants of the 7th Assault Gun Battalion, the Group launched a counter-attack at Baracska-Petend on December 7.

On March 8, the 20th Assault Gun Battalion (15 Hetzers) and the 25th Reconnaissance Battalion fought together with the German 4th Cavalry Division near Lake Balaton. The 25th Infantry Regiment, supported by the 20th Assault Gun Battalion, reclaimed Enyig during March 9-11.

During World War II, the Armoured Troops alone suffered 3305 causalities just from June 26, 1941 to October 31, 1944.

Armoured Trains

In 1920, the Hungarian Army had 9 armoured trains that were remnants of the k. und k. Army of the World War I period. Because of the dictates of the Treaty of Trianon, the armoured trains were disassembled and stored in secret caches. In 1929 the Ministry of Defence re-evaluated these trains and decommissioned five of them due to their poor condition. The four that remained in the best shape were modernised and reintroduced into service.

They were numbered I-IV, and in 1932 renumbered 1-4. In 1938 they were again modernised. The main armaments of the trains were 80mm 5/8m and 18M guns. From 1932 to 1934, the Rába Vp. armoured car was converted to a rail armoured car. The trains were renumbered as follows:

101. High coach armed with one 80mm and one 37mm gun, two 20mm anti-tank guns and six 8mm machine-guns.

102. Flat coach, same armaments as 101.

103. High coach, same armaments as 101.

104. Self-propelled one coach, armed with one 80mm gun and one 20 mm AT gun and two 8mm machine-guns.

As of 1940, the armoured trains were used as independent companies under the direct command of the General Staff, each company having one steam engine, two fortified coaches and two flat cars, plus a supply train.

The trains participated in operations as follows:

– 1938: Nos. 101 and 102 took part in the recovery of Upper Hungary

– 1939: all the trains were involved in the occupation of Carpathian-Ukraine

– 1940: all the trains were involved in the Transylvania action, but only No. 102 entered the region

– 1941: all the trains took part in the action against Yugoslavia

During the Russian campaign, use of the armoured trains was limited by track gauge; however the Hungarian Occupation Forces in the Ukraine used captured Russian armoured trains. Occupation Group East used such a train against partisans at Bryansk during 1942 - 1944. Occupation Group West used a captured former Polish armoured train in Upper Hungary, where it was abandoned in 1944.

Armoured trains 101-104 all took part in the battles for the defence of Hungary. The 102nd Armoured Train supported the advancing 2nd Army in Transylvania and captured an important railroad bridge at Marosbogát, deep behind the Romanian lines, on September 6, 1944. The bridge was successfully held until the

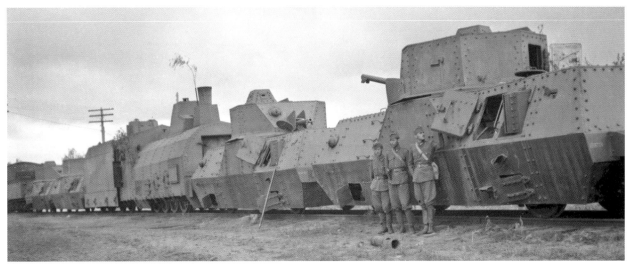

The Hungarian Occupation Forces operated captured, ex Polish and Soviet armoured trains to secure the rail network behind the front. Ex-Soviet armoured train with Hungarian crew in Ukraine. [Fortepan 107619]

arrival of the 2nd Armoured Division. In late 1944 early 1945, the trains were involved in the fighting around Budapest and at Lake Balaton.

CHAPTER VI

Production of the Hungarian Armoured vehicles

The Defence Industry in Hungary

Following the end of World War I, Hungarian military industry was in bad shape. The lost resources of her territories ceded to other nations, manpower losses caused by the war, and the limitations imposed by the Treaty of Trianon all played their part in this situation. During the late 1920s and early 1930s, the economic situation of the country began to improve. Hungary's economy was essentially based on agriculture, and those industries which existed did so mainly to provide tools and equipment meant for use in agriculture.

However, a small number of famous heavy industrial companies which originated in the old k. und k. period played a very important role in the military industry. From the 1930s, the Manfred Weiss, FÉG, Diósgyőri State Weapon Factory, Ganz, MÁVAG, Magyar Vagon és Gépgyár (Rába), GAMMA, and

Hungarian designed V-4 light tank on evaluation training in 1938, the armament of the tank was up to the standard in late 30s, and however the armour protection and mobility was not. [Sárhidai Gyula]

Danuvia companies provided the backbone to the Hungarian military industry. Due to financial constraints, these companies initially focused on repairs and modifications to existing equipment, but later worked on production under license and independent developments.

Production of Armoured Vehicles

The Manfred Weiss, Ganz, MAVAG, and Magyar Vagon és Gépgyár (Rába) factories were able to preserve and later expand their skills and capacities to produce armour for the Hungarian

38. M Toldi light tanks advance in the cover of smoke on an exercise in 1941. The tanks have three tone camouflage and octagonal military insignia and Mechanised Branch sign on their turrets. [Mujzer Péter]

The Hungarian Army held a big scale military parade for Admiral Horthy and for the political and military elite at Kolozsvár on 10 September 1940. The Army presented its most modern weapons, the brand new 38. M Toldi light tank passing the tribune. The Toldis just arrived to the troops before the operation. [MFI]

Hungarian light tank company with 38. M Toldi tanks, at the main street of Kolomea, in July 1941. The crews wear mechanic's overalls, on the street are Hungarian and Ukrainian flags. [Mujzer Péter]

38. M Toldi light tank advancing through a burned down Ukrainian town is summer of 1941. The stiff Soviet resistance surprised the Hungarians too. [Mujzer Péter]

Army. Of course, in the early 1930s any work and development carried out had to be done in secret.

Having procured and tested the Fiat Ansaldo tankettes, the Hungarian military recognised that modern mobile-armoured tactics called for vehicles that were more powerful than these tankettes. Ideally a more powerful light tank was needed, but no such vehicle was being produced in Hungary and the Trianon Treaty precluded the purchase of foreign tanks. However, a Hungarian firm, the Manfred Weiss Company, offered a prototype of a light tank which was code-named V-3 (vontató = tractor) to conceal the real identity of the vehicle and its purpose.

According to the original title of the photo "the Creek of Makirowka cannot stop our tank". The 38.M Toldi has octagonal military insignia and Mechanised Branch sign belonged to the armoured troops of the Mobile Corps in summer of 1941. [Mujzer Péter]

Advancing troops of the 1. Cavalry Brigade, the trucks and light tanks moving on the "highway ", the cavalry and horsed drawn wagons advancing next to the road on the fields. The 38. M Toldi light tanks role at the armoured cavalry battalions was to reinforce the tankette companies. [Mujzer Péter]

V-3, V-4 Light Tanks

In 1933, engineer Mike Straussler, who worked for the Manfred Weiss Company, presented a plan to the Army Staff for a special light tank which could move on tracks and wheels and which was also amphibious. This idea was supported by the Army and the turretless body was completed in 1936 to be used as a basis for further developments. The same year a complete and more advanced version, the V-4 was built. Two tanks were produced; one for export and another for test trials by the Hungarian Army. In 1937 the test trials were carried out and some new requirements were imposed by the Army, the installation of a twin-machine gun in the turret, and enlargement of the crew from three to four.

The modified V-4 was presented in 1938, but the tests were unsuccessful due to some basic problems. It was judged that the body shape was too high and unstable, and the engine was under-powered. The V-4 was tested by the Ministry of Defence against the Swedish L-60. The Swedish tank performed better overall, and the Army Staff supported the purchase of a licence to manufacture the L-60.

The Italian Army shown interest towards the V-4 light tank. In 1937, the prototype with three men crew and armed only with gun was transported to Italy, tested by the Italians. However, it was not accepted by the Italian Army and was transported back to Hungary in 1942. The first prototype of the Hungarian designed and produced armoured vehicle was left at a military store, Budafok Háros and most probably captured by the Red Army units in 1945.

Technical Data

Designation: **V-4 light tank**
Year of production: 1938
Factory/produced quantity: Weis Manfred Factory, 2. prototype
Combat weight: 12,7 t
Length: 4700 mm
Width: 2850 mm
Height: 2575 mm
Ground pressure: 0,56 kp/cm/3
Crew: 4
Engine: WM A.C. II
Displacement: 7240 cm/3
Cylinders: 8
Horsepower: 200 Hp
Speed:
– on tracks: 32 km/h,
– on wheels: 46 km/h,
– on water: 6 km/h
Obstacle – step: 0,6 m
– ditch: 1,4 m
– ford: 0,8 m
Armament:
– one 37M 40 mm gun;
– two twin 34M A 8 mm machine-guns
Armour:
26 - 9 mm

Home coming parade of the Mobil Corps was held on 14 December 1941 at Budapest. Most of the parading vehicles were collected from other units, because the Mobile Corps lost most of its vehicles. 38. M Toldi tanks parading on the Andrassy Boulevard. [Mujzer Péter]

38. M Toldi light tank equipped with stick antenna, the crew wears the woollen sleeve leather jerkin, a practical piece of uniform and the 37. M leather crash helmet, at River Don 1942. [Mujzer Péter]

A few 38. M Toldi light tank served at the 3. Tank Regiment in September 1944, the tank commander has the intercom in his hand. [Fortepan 20389]

Factory fresh 38. M Toldi light tanks at the Automobile Depot of the Army, wait for transfer to the troops. The tanks painted in dark olive green camouflage. [Fortepan 72118, Lissák Tivadar]

38. M Toldi light tank belongs to the Light Tank Company of the 1. Armoured Cavalry battalion, wears the unit insignia painted on the turret hatch and the side of the vehicle. The unit sign was a white Turul bird with sword. [Mujzer Péter]

38. M Toldi tanks on training in 1943-1944, the 36. M 20mm anti-tank rifles removed from the turret, the vehicles have the late style military insignia. [Szollár János]

38. M Toldi II light tank armed with 40 mm gun, in dark olive green camouflage, during the operation in Transylvania, September 1944. [Karai Sándor]

38. M Toldi Light Tanks

The L-60 Landsverk was introduced in Hungary in 1937. The MAVAG Company, supported by the Ministry of Defence, purchased a sample and ran it through a series of competitive trials with the V-4. The trials of the L-60 led the Army Staff commission to recommend that:
– the steering configuration be changed,
– the transmission be modernised,
– more extensive vision devices be added,
– the ventilation be improved,
– the suspension be modified for a smoother ride.

The commission recommended that four squadrons be equipped, each with 16 tanks, for each of the four mobile brigades. The licence to build the L-60 was purchased by the MÁVAG and Ganz Companies. The Swedish tank was designated the 38. M Toldi I light tank. The Ministry of Defence ordered 40 tanks from each company in February 1939.

The Toldi light tank was almost 100% the same as the original L-60 except for the armament. Based on the recomendation of the Military Technical Institute (HTI), the 20 mm 36. M anti-tank rifle with one 8 mm 34/37. AM co-axial machine gun was adopted for the Toldi tanks.

The Hungarian Army hoped and planned to build the tanks entirely in Hungary to avoid foreign interference. However, because of insufficient preparation, the first 80 Toldi tanks were built using some components supplied by Sweden and Germany.

After the first 80 vehicles, the Ministry of Defence ordered a second series of tanks which were designated the Toldi II due to some slight modifications. This meant that the Toldi light tank became a 100% home-produced vehicle in 1940. The MAVAG Company began producing the German Bussing NAG engine, the Ganz Company produced the transmission, and the Ruggyantagyár Company manufactured the rubber wheel rims.

There were some difficulties in reaching agreement with MÁVAG and Ganz concerning suitable payment for the vehicles. The mixture of foreign and domestic parts also created many serious problems and resulting production delays.

In April 1939 the R-5 radio (built by the Hungarian Standard Company) was adapted for use on the Toldis. The Toldi I used the R-5 with arched shape radio mast and the Toldi II had an R-5/a with stick radio mast.

Additional modifications had to be made to the turret in order to mount the selected anti-tank rifle and machine gun. The first two Toldi tanks, with serial numbers H-301 and H-302

38. M Toldi light tank decorated with garlands on display. The tank has the octagonal military insignia. [Fortepan 43999]

Closer look of the 38. M Toldi on an Army exhibition, surrounded by curious civilians and nuns. The bright octagonal military insignia well visible. [Fortepan 78326]

were completed and assigned to the 2nd Motorised Rifle Brigade in April 1940.

However, the building program fell behind schedule and by June 1940 there were only 20 Toldis produced, and not all were fully equipped with armaments and periscopes. By September 1940, only 45 Toldi tanks had been delivered to armoured units; by October of that year the number had grown to around 72.

By June 1941, 85 Toldi tanks were completed in total, those from MAVAG bearing the serial numbers H301-340 and H381-385, and those from Ganz bearing the numbers H340-380.

From 1941, the Hungarian industries were able to produce Toldi tanks without the need for imported parts. 110 Toldi II

tanks were ordered, 68 of them (H423-490) manufactured by Ganz and 42 (H381-422) by MAVAG.

By the end of 1942, total production of the Toldi I and II tanks had reached 190 vehicles. However, the initial experiences in war had revealed the disadvantages of the Toldi: inadequate main armament and weak armour. The Military Technical Institute (HTI) began designing an improved version to satisfy the new requirements. The new vehicle had additional armour on the front of the hull and on the turret, and was to be armed with a 40 mm gun. Two prototypes were completed but production was delayed due to work on rebuilding the earlier Toldi tanks and work on the Turán program.

38. M Toldi light tank belonged one of the bicycle-tank battalion advancing in a Ukrainian village. The tank painted in three tones camouflage wearing octagonal military insignia. [Fortepan 78326]

38. M Toldi light advancing in the same Ukrainian village. The reflector protection cover is open, the 34/37. M machine gun missing from the turret. [Fortepan 78327]

38. M Toldi light tank wearing the early, Maltese cross military insignia, exclusively used by the 1. Reconnaissance Battalion's vehicles. The photo taken in 1942 during a tank familiarisation course held for infantry. [Fortepan 107718]

38. M Toldi light tank on cooperation exercise with the infantry in early 1942, prior to the deployment of 2. Hungarian Army to the front. However the Toldi tank was not able to prepare the Hungarian infantry to handle the Soviet T-34 tanks. [Fortepan 107719]

Armoured officers standing in front of a 38. M Toldi light tank wearing the two pieces leather protective gear with Italian style crash helmet between them a nicely dressed lady and an officer in duty uniform at Jászberény, 1/II Tank Battalion. [Szollár János]

38. M Toldi light tank and a captured Lt. vz. 35 ex-Slovakian tank facing each other, the size differences are clearly visible, in favour to the Lt. vz. 35. [Szollár János]

Advancing German infantry and Hungarian 38. M Toldi light tank belonged to the Mobile Corps during the operation in Yugoslavia, Voivodina April 1941. Thec34/37. M 8mm machine gun is on AA mount. [Jean-Francois Antoina]

German despatch rider and Hungarian armoured troops standing in front of a 38. M Toldi light tank during the Yugoslavian Campaign. [Jean-Francois Antoina]

Advancing 38. M Toldi light tank passing a German horse drawn column in Voivodina, April 1941. The tank commander has a crash helmet with intercom.[Jean-Francois Antoina]

Production of the 43M Toldi III began at Ganz in the autumn of 1943 but there is no record of how many, if any, were delivered to the armoured troops.

In 1942 the troops had 80 Toldi II tanks with totally inadequate armament, so plans were made to re-arm some with the 42. M 40 mm gun as used on the Toldi III. The new gun performed much better against tanks, being able to penetrate 30mm armour from 1000 meters, however by 1944 this too proved to be inadequate. Due to the size of the weapon, the turret was modified. A metal box was attached to the rear of the turret to give better stability, the armour was increased and the torsion was strengthened. The 80 tanks so modified were

Hungarian 38. M Toldi light tank moves on the street of Vukovár, small town in Voivodina, April 1941. The crew wear filed cap instead of crash helmet. [Jean –Francois Antoina]

38. M Toldi light tank, number plate H-321, 1. Reconnaissance Battalion, unit sign, white lightning bolt painted on the right mudguard. [Mujzer Péter]

38. M Toldi light tank belongs to the 1. Reconnaissance Battalion entering in to a Transylvanian town, in September 1940. The rear number plate, H-320 was painted on a white square. [Mujzer Péter]

designated Toldi II A. As of October 1, 1943 the armoured forces had 96 Toldi T20 and 80 Toldi T40 tanks.

Based on German experience, the HTI also experimented with a skirting-plated Toldi tank in 1943. An up-gunned Toldi II A was covered with 5-8 mm additional armour plates but tests showed that this did not provide better protection but merely increased the weight by 500 kg.

Battlefield experiences highlighted the lack of armoured medical vehicles. In 1942 the 30th Tank Regiment successfully used three Toldi II for transporting medical crews close

The 34/37. M machine gun of the 38. M Toldi light tank removed from the turret and put on AA mountings. However the 25 round magazine and lack of AA sight made the machine gun inadequate for this role. [Mujzer Péter]

38. M Toldi light tank platoon of the 1. Reconnaissance Battalion entering into a Transylvanian village in September 1940. The position of the three man crew is seen on the photo. [Mujzer Péter]

Curious Hungarian children in their best traditional cloths sitting on the 38. M Toldi light tank during the celebration given by the local Hungarian population in a Transylvanian town. [Mujzer Péter]

Troop commander sitting on the turret of the 38. M Toldi light tank, the 34/37. M machine gun on AA mounting. The metal plate covering the machine gun on the front of the turret is open for ventilation. [Mujzer Péter]

to damaged tanks to evacuate injured personnel from the battle field. The HTI recommended the modification of a few Toldi I tanks for medical duties. In March 1944 nine Toldi I were modified at Ganz. The left side hatch was enlarge to ease boarding casualties and the amount of ammunition carried was reduced and instead of ammunition boxes, medical materials were kept in the turret. The nine medical vehicles, named 43. M Toldi medical light tanks, were handed over to the troops in June - July 1944.

One Toldi I was modified by Ganz in February 1944 as a tank hunter, with a 75 mm gun mounted in an open compartment. This experimental version was similar to the German Marder vehicle. The Hungarian troops fought with 7 leased German Marder tank hunter in 1943 at River Don. One Marder survived the operation and return to Hungary with the Hungarian troop. The HTI used the Marder to rebuilt the Hungarian version of it on the platform of the Toldi light tank.

38. M Toldi light tank on flat car transported back to Hungary after the occupation of Transylvania. The octagonal military insignia and the Mechanised Branch sign is on the turret. [Mujzer Péter]

The open turret hatches of the 38. M Toldi light tank, the tools attached to the rear of the hull. The crew has crash helmet with intercom, the radio antenna in transmitting position. [Mujzer Péter]

38. M Toldi light tank belong to the 1. Reconnaissance Battalion with new octagonal military insignia and white lightning bolt unit sign. The tank guarding a Hungarian HQ in Voivodina 1941. [Mujzer Péter]

Prototype of the 40mm gun 38. M Toldi II light tank on the yard of MÁVAG Factory. The gun in the Toldi II was original invented and used at the V-4 light tank. [Sárhidai Gyula]

Experimental skirt plated 38. M Toldi II light tank at the MÁVAG Factory. The skirt plates add an extra 500 kg to the weight of the vehicle. [Sárhidai Gyula]

However, project was aborted due to the increased weight, the long barrel gun which reduced the manoeuvrability and the stability. The Germans were not interested in providing PaK 40 anti-tank guns either.

The last modification of the 38. M Toldi light tank was done in summer of 1944. The Hungarian designed anti-tank rocket launcher 44. M Buzogány (Maul) system was installed on the hull, behind the turret.

This project was hidden until recently when a strange photo emerged on the internet. The photo was taken by an US sergeant belonged to the 691. Tank Destroyer Battalion,

Driving panel and steering wheel of the 38. M Toldi light tank. [Sárhidai Gyula]

38. M Toldi tank turret left side interior, with the 20mm 36. M anti-tank rifle and the 34/37. M 8mm machine gun. [Sárhidai Gyula]

38. M Toldi tank turret right side interior, with the 20mm 36. M anti-tank rifle. The interior of the Hungarian armoured vehicles was painted white. [Sárhidai Gyula]

3. US Army, in April-May 1945, somewhere in Bavaria. So far we have no documents about the weapon system, nor the installation, neither the location where the photo was taken. On the other hand recently another photo emerged on the installation of the Buzogány anti-tank rocket system on Zrínyi assault howitzer.

Technical Data

Designation: **38. M Toldi I (light tank A20) and Toldi II (light tank B20)**
Years of production: 1939-1940
Factory/produced quantity: Ganz /108, MÁVAG /82
Number plates:
– Toldi I: H-301-H-381
– ToldiII: H-382- H-490
Combat weight: 8,5 t
Length: 4750 mm
Width: 2140 mm
Height: 2020 mm
Ground pressure: 0,5kp /cm/3
Crew: 3
Engine Bussing NAG type L8 V/36 Tr
Displacement: 7913 cm/3
Cylinders: 8
Horsepower: 155 Hp
Max. Speed: 50 km/h
Range: 200 km
Obstacle:
– step: 0,6 m
– ditch: 1,75 m
– ford: 0,7 m
Armament:
– one 36. M 20 mm anti-tank rifle;
– one 34/37. M 8 mm machine-gun
Ammunition:
– 208 20mm shell, 52 magazines
– 2400 8mm rounds 96 magazines
Armour: 5-13 mm
Radio:
– Toldi I R-5 radio with arc antenna
– Toldi II R-5/a with stick antenna

Designation: **38. M Toldi IIA (light tank B40)**
Years of production: 1942-1944
Factory/ produced quantity: Ganz/ 80
Combat weight: 9,35 t
Length: 4750 mm

The 34/37. M 8 mm machine gun used for the 38. M Toldi I light tank, the machine gun had just 25 rounds magazine, later it was redesigned for belt fed system. [Sárhidai Gyula]

Width: 2100 mm
Height: 2020 mm
Ground pressure: 0,547 kp/cm/3
Crew: 3
Engine Bussing NAG Type L8V/36 Tr
Displacement: 7913 cm/3
Cylinders: 8
Horsepower: 155 Hp
Max. Speed: 47 km/h
Range: 190 km
Obstacle:
– step: 0,60 m
– ditch: 1,75 m
– ford: 0,70 m
Armament:
– one 37/42. M 40 mm L/26 gun;
– maximum firing range: 8400 m
– rate of fire: 15-16 rounds /minute
– one 34/40. AM 8 mm machinegun
Ammunition:
– 55 40 mm 36. M armoured piercing or 39. M fragmentation shell
– 3200 8mm cartridge
Armour: 35-13 mm
Radio: R-5/a with stick antenna
Designation: **43. M Toldi IIIA (light tank C40) prototype**
Years of production: 1942-1943
Factory: HTI/Ganz
Number plate: H-483
Combat weight: 9,45 t

38. M Toldi light tank turret, with open left hatch, the gunner aiming the 36. M 20mm anti-tank rifle with telescopic sight. [Mujzer Péter]

38. M Toldi light tanks belong to the Ludovika Academy Armoured Class, the traditional Ludovika unit sign painted on the turret. [Mujzer Péter]

Length: 4750 mm
Width: 2140 mm
Height: 2070 mm
Ground pressure: 0,61 kp/cm/3
Crew: 3
Engine Ganz VIII VGT.107
Displacement: 7913 cm/3
Cylinders: 8
Horsepower: 155 Hp
Max. Speed: 45 km/h
Range: 190 km
Obstacle:
– step: 0,60 m
– ditch: 1,75 m
– ford: 0,70 m
Armament:
– one 42. M 40 mm gun
– one 34/40. AM 8 mm machine-gun
Ammunition:
– 87 36. M armoured piercing and 39. M fragmentation shell
– 3200 8mm cartridge
Armour: 35-6 mm
Radio: R-5/a radio with stick antenna

40. M Nimród anti-tank/anti-aircraft vehicle

The Hungarian military acknowledged the need for motorised and armoured units in the field to have some kind of air and anti-tank defence. Hungary already had the licence to produce the L-60 (Toldi) tank, and this facilitated the adoption, after test trials by the Hungarian mobile troops, of the L-62. Hungary had purchased one of these Swedish vehicles, without armament, in 1939.

The licence for the L-62 was purchased by MAVAG in 1940 and the vehicle was officially designated the 40. M Nimród self-propelled A/A-AT vehicle. The original structure was modified to enlarge the turret for a four-man crew, and the 36. M 40 mm Bofors gun built under licence by MÁVAG was mounted on it.

The Nimród was very similar to the Toldi except it had a longer hull, with five road wheels and three return rollers. It was produced with a Ganz Bussing NAG engine and Hungarian-made suspension and transmission. The open-top turret was sloped and roomy, and the gun mantel was designed for maximum elevation and traverse of the Bofors gun. The turret

40. M Nimród Sp. AT/AA vehicles of the 51. Sp. AT/AA Battalion and Skoda 38(t) tanks of the 1. Armoured Field Division on parade before deployment to the front in April 1942. The Nimróds painted in three tones camouflage with large octagonal military insignia. [Mujzer Péter]

40. M Nimród Sp. AT/AA vehicles on display at the Automobile Depot, the Nimród has three tone camouflage and large military insignia on the engine deck for air recognition. [Fortepan 72097, Lissák Tivadar]

40. M Nimród Sp. AT/AA vehicles on display at the Automobile Depot, the Nimród has three tone camouflage. [Fortepan 72097, Lissák Tivadar]

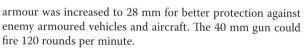

40. M Nimród Sp. AT/AA vehicles on display at the Automobile Depot, the Nimród has three tone camouflage and late style military insignia on the side. [Fortepan 72097]

40. M Nimród Sp. AT/AA vehicles on display at the Automobile Depot, in front of the Nimród the Bussing NAG TypeL8 V636 Tr. engines. [Fortepan 72097, Lissák Tivadar]

armour was increased to 28 mm for better protection against enemy armoured vehicles and aircraft. The 40 mm gun could fire 120 rounds per minute.

In 1940 the Ministry of Defence ordered 46 Nimróds (H050-095) and in 1941 a further 89 vehicles (1H630-718) were requested from the MÁVAG factory.

The first Nimród saw action in 1942, but it quickly became apparent that it was inadequate against the Russian T-34 and KV tanks due to its light armament, high silhouette, and thin armour. However, it was used successfully during the war for anti-aircraft duties.

During the latter stages of the war, in 1944-45, the Nimród received the 42M "Kerngranate" (rocket grenade launcher) to

40. M Nimród Sp AT/AA vehicle on firing exercise, the vehicle had a high profile which made it easy target. Late stage of the war the Nimróds used mainly in air defence role. [Mujzer Péter]

40. M Nimróds Sp. AT/AA vehicles and one 36. M Bofors 40mm AA gun on firing exercise. The Nimróds were also armed with the 40mm 36. M Bofors gun. [Fortepan 43951]

The Nimród's crew preparing the 40mm shells of the Nimród Sp.AT/AA vehicle for ready to use, loading 4 shells into metal clips. [Fortepan 43952]

increase its armour-piercing capability. The disadvantage of this "Kerngranate" was that the crew had to leave the vehicle to put the grenade in the barrel, so it was used only in ambush positions.

To fill a need, the HTI designed an armoured personnel and medical carrier based on the Nimród chassis. This vehicle was designated the 43. M Lehel. The turret was replaced by a low open-top superstructure. However, only one example was produced. It was planned to use the Lehel as an armoured ambulance vehicle and assault engineer carrier, but due to the higher priority of other programs (Turán, Zrínyi), production was cancelled.

40. M Nimród Sp.AT/AA vehicle climbing the steep terrain, the shape of the turret can be seen on this picture. The armour only protects against small arms and fragments. [Fortepan 43955]

Vehicle maintenance of the 40. M Nimród Sp.AT/AA vehicle, the unit sign of the 51. Sp.AT/AA Battalion is on the back of the vehicles, inside a white rhombus a horseman. [Fortepan 43959]

Senior NCO in winter great coat with sword stands in front of 40. M Nimróds vehicles parking in a depot of the 51. Sp.AT/AA Battalion. [Fortepan 43982]

Nimród company of 51. Sp.AT/AA Battalion in air defence positon alongside the road in 1942, the 40mm guns put in high elevation, among the vehicles is a range finder. [Fortepan 43995]

Nimród company on driving exercise, belonged to the 51. Sp.AT/AA Battalion, the octagonal military insignia painted on the turret and at the front of the vehicle. [Fortepan 43997]

Curious villagers climbed on the 40. M Nimród Sp.AT/AA vehicles during a short rest in 1942, the number plate H-070. Any motorised vehicles at that time was magic for the rural Hungary. [Fortepan 44001]

Range finder and 40. M Nimród Sp.AT/AA vehicle on a firing exercise, the vehicle has the three tone camouflage. [Fortepan 44006]

Bird view of turret of the 40. M Nimród vehicle, the crowded position of the 4 men gun crew clearly seen. The photo was taken after the war in Hungary. [Sárhidai Gyula]

Advancing 40. M Nimród Sp. AT/AA vehicle of the 51. Sp.AT/AA Battalion passing a typical Ukrainian village at River Don, summer of 1944. [Mujzer Péter]

Technical Data

Designation: **40. M Nimród anti-tank/ anti-aircraft vehicle**
Years of production: 1940 – 1944
Factory/produced quantity: MÁVAG /135
Combat weight: 10.5t
Length: 5750 mm / 5323 mm (with/without barrel)
Width: 2300 mm
Height: 2840 mm
Ground pressure: 0,60 kp/cm/3
Crew: 6
Engine: Bussing NAG Type L8 V636 Tr.
Displacement: 7913 cm/3
Cylinders: 8
Horsepower: 155 Hp
Speed: 46,5 km/h
Range: 200 km
Obstacle:
– step: 0,6 – 0,8 m
– ditch: 2-2,2 m
– ford: 0,70 m
Armaments:
– onc 36. M 40 mm Bofors gun
– maximum range: 4600 m
– rate of fire: 120 rounds/minute
Crew self-protection weapons: three 39. M submachine gun and two 31. M rifle
Ammunition: 160 40mm shell
Armour: 13-6 mm
Radio: R-5/a with stick antenna
Number plates:
– I. series H-055 – H-100
– II. series 1H-630 – 1H-718

Designation: **43. M Lehel medical vehicle / troop carrier prototype**
Years of production: 1943
Factory/produced quantity: HTI/MÁVAG
Combat weight: 10,2 t
Length: 5320 mm
Width: 2140 mm
Height: 1800 mm
Ground pressure: 0,56 kp/cm/3
Crew: 1 + 8
Engine: Bussing NAG Type L8 V/36 Tr.
Displacement: 7913 cm/3
Cylinders: 8
Horsepower: 155 Hp

40. M Nimród Sp. AT/AA vehicle with probably the unit sign of an AA platoon belongs to a motorised rifle battalion. The unit sign also painted on the garage door. [Mujzer Péter]

Another view of the 40. M Nimród painted in dark olive gree with late style military insignia. [Mujzer Péter]

Speed: 50 km/h
Range: 225 km
Obstacle:
– step: 0,6 -0,8 m
– ditch: 2 -2,2 m
– ford: 0,8 m
Armaments:
– one 31. M 8 mm light machine-gun
– two 39. M submachine gun
Ammunition:
– 1500 8mm cartridge
– 2 x 560 9 mm cartridge
Armour: 7-20 mm
Radio: R-5/a with stick antenna

A close view of the 40. M Nimród, the open driver hatch, it was called helmet can be seen. [Mujzer Péter]

Cleaning the 40. M Nimród Sp.AT/AA vehicles in the barrack's yard, next to the Nimród is a wheeled filed kitchen, so called "goulash canon". [Fortepan]

The gunners of the 40. M Nimród Sp.AT/AA vehicles worn 35. M steel helmet in the open top turret of the vehicle. [Bonhardt Attila]

Right side view of the 40. M Nimród Sp.AT/AA vehicle with large octagonal military insignia and three tones camouflage. [Sárhidai Gyula]

Top view of the 40. M Nimród Sp.AT/AA vehicles, the distribution of the octagonal military insignias at front, both side of the turret and on the engine deck visible. The four men gun crew position is also seen on the photo. [Sárhidai Gyula]

40. M Turán Medium Tank

At the end of the 1930s it became obvious that the tankettes and light tanks used by the Hungarian Army were unsuitable as battle tanks. The question remained of where the Hungarians could purchase suitable medium or heavy tanks to equip the planned tank divisions. At that time Sweden and Italy had no suitable models, and the Germans rejected Hungarian proposals to purchase production licences.

In 1939, the MÁVAG and Ganz factories negotiated with Landsverk to purchase the licence to build the heavy LAGO tank (15 t, 47 mm gun), but the negotiations were unsuccessful.

40. M Turán medium tanks with three tones camouflage, late style military insignia stay at the yard of the Automobile Depot of the Army, before distribution to the units. [Fortepan 72260, Lissák Tivadar]

40. M Turán tanks are at the maintenance workshop of the Depot. The WM V-8H engine removed from the hull and rest next to the tank. One of the tank has a four digits turret number, just the three first digit is visible, 412?. On the building structure is a funny slogan, "Keep smiling". (Fortepan 72226, Lissák Tivadar)

The yard of the Automobile Depot, a captured Soviet BT-7 is next to the 40. M Turán medium tank. It is interesting to recognise that the two tanks are similar in size. However the late 30s Soviet model has a much powerful gun than the Turán. [Fortepan 72493, Lissák Tibor]

Abandoned 40. M Turán medium tank, turret number 3012, belonged to the battalion staff of the 3/III Tank Battalion. The photo was taken in Hungary, summer of 1945. [Mujzer Péter]

The propaganda also utilised the armour production, a 40. M Turán medium tank played in a Hungarian romantic comedy which was never finished. [Fortepan]

40. M medium Turán tank hull and turret waits in the yard to be finished, in the Ganz Factory, Budapest 1942. [Bonhardt Attila]

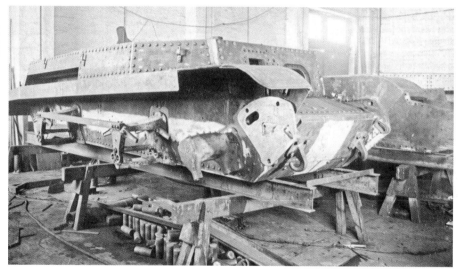

Side view of the Turán's hull rests on the assembly line in the Ganz Factory, Budapest 1942. [Bonhardt Attila]

The only solution seemed to be the former Czechoslovakian Skoda Company; a list of licences for sale was made available to Hungary in late 1939. The Hungarians had had good experiences with Czech military industry products during the k. und k. era.

Furthermore, in 1939 two Czech LT-35 tanks had been captured by Hungarian troops and handed over to the HTI for testing, with positive results. On the list of available licences was the T-21 tank, which was seen as a possible solution as a medium tank for the Hungarian military. After complex test trials in Hajmáskér, the Hungarians requested some modifications:
– increasing the armour to 35 mm,
– replacing the command cupola by a fixed one,
– replacing the electrical equipment with Bosch products,
– mounting a 40 mm gun instead of 47 mm.

The reason for reducing the gun calibre was that the new Hungarian 40 mm gun had a muzzle velocity of 820 m/s instead of 590 m/s for the 47mm gun. It also fired the 36. M 40 mm shell, which was used for the Bofors. The licence was sold to Hungary in July 1940. Hungary agreed to manufacture the Turán tanks only for her own use and not for export. The Turán program was farmed out to four companies: Manfred Weiss, MÁVAG, Ganz and Győri Magyar Vagon és Gépgyár. The plan was to produce 230 40. M Turán medium tanks for the two divisions that were being created.

The 40. M Turán was produced in two versions, a command version with one R-5 and two R-4 radios, and the combat version with just one R-5 and one R-4 radio. Of course the command version had reduced ammunition capacity. The organisation of the joint manufacturing program was very complicated and very slow. During the initial stages of mass production, about 200 different modifications were done to the original plans because the original prototype was found to be flawed. The first prototype Turán was finished in June 1941. During testing of the iron prototype new problems arose: the engine overheated, and additional problems were found with the gearbox and chassis. A new radiator was designed by Manfred Weiss which overcame the problems.

Another problem was the armour plating. Until then, Hungarian steel mills had manufactured armour plating only up to a thickness of 13 mm. The steel mill in Diósgyőr developed a new type MESTER plate and Magyar Vagon és Gépgyár also developed the AJAX plate; these were more resistant to penetration but were somewhat brittle. The frontal armour was increased to 50 mm, but because of the lack of proper plates this was achieved by combining a 25 mm and 35 mm plate.

Because of all these problems, the first vehicles did not leave the factories until the summer of 1942. A combination of badly-

40M Turán repaired at the Depot; on the wall we can see encouraging slogans which intended to improve the morel of the staff. The spare wheels and smoke candles attached to the rear of the tank. [Fortepan 72516, Lissák Tivadar]

40. M Turán medium tank belonged to the Ludovika Accademy, the sign of the Academy painted on the turret. The drivers were conscripted men, the rest of the crew were officer candidates. [Éder Miklós]

The mascot, a Hungarian Pulli dog of an unidentified unit sit next to the open turret side hatch of the 40. M Turán tank. [Éder Miklós]

Internal photo of the 40. M Turán commander's station with radio equipment and the turret side hatch. [Éder Miklós]

40. M Turán medium tank at the barrack's yard. The complicated Skoda style running gear system can be seen. [Szollár János]

40. M Turán medium tank on all terrain driving exercise. The turret side hatch is open, the crew are hanging out of the open hatches wearing field caps instead of crash helmet. [Szollár János]

Another view of the 40. M Turán medium tank, four out of five men crew just hanging outside of the tank. [Szollár János]

40. M Turán medium tank with its commander, entrenching tools attached to the hull. [Szollár János]

Abandoned 40. M Turán tanks somewhere in Galicia winter of 1944/45 after the end of the battles. The Turán tank in the front with skirt plates on the turrets, was prepared for towing, but left behind, the turret weapons removed by the Soviet forces for evaluation. [Szollár János]

40. M Turán medium tank belongs to the Ludovika Academy is presenting an obstacle course for high ranking officers. The engine deck, the exhausting pipes, the spare wheels and between them the smoke candles can be seen. [Éder Miklós]

Close look of the right rear section of the Turán tank, the exhausting pipe and the spare wheel can be seen. [Sárhidai Gyula]

The pride of the Hungarian Armoured Forces, the 41. M Turán heavy tanks wait at the Automobile Depot of the Army for distribution to the troops. The tanks have the three tones camouflage. [Fortepan 72449, Lissák Tivadar]

trained drivers, insufficient maintenance and the short training program created a lot of problems for this first Turán series.

The first Turáns were delivered to the Armoured Training School at Esztergom in July 1942. The 1/I, 2/I, 3/I, 4/I Tank Battalions were equipped with their Turáns at the end of 1942. A total of 230 Turáns were produced by the end of 1942.

A second order for 309 40. M Turán tanks were placed, but due to the development of the new heavy Turáns, only 55 were manufactured. Experience on the Eastern Front had clearly shown that the tankettes and light tanks were useless as decisive weapons, and also that any tank with a gun smaller than 75 mm was ineffective against Russian armour.

41. M Turán Heavy Tank

In 1941 the General Staff ordered a new heavy tank based on the medium Turán. Although this new tank was considered as heavy by Hungarian standards, in fact it was basically a version of the 40. M Turán medium tank with increased armament and additional armour. The prototype of the heavy Turán was finished in 1942, but production did not begin until early 1943.

41. M Turán heavy tanks loaded on flatcars at Budafokháros railway station, captured by the Red Army at the siege of Budapest, spring of 1945. The Turán tanks protection upgraded with perforated skirt plates. [Szollár János]

Close look of the 8mm hull machine gun of the Turán tank, the hull of the 40. and 41. M tanks were identical to each other. [Sárhidai Gyula]

The main armament of the 41. M Turán heavy tank was the 7,5cm short barrelled gun. It was developed from a WWI artillery piece, which clearly was ineffective against the Soviet medium tanks. [Sárhidai Gyula]

The turret machine gun of the 41. M Turán medium ctank, the turret protection was added with skirt plate and spare tracks put between the skirt plate and the turret. It reflects on the fact how weak was the armour plate of the Turán tanks. [Sárhidai Gyula]

The main armament of the 41. M heavy Turán was a short-barrelled gun which had a muzzle velocity of 500 m/sec, which was supposed to be effective against 50 mm vertical armour plate at a range of 500 m. The armour plating was increased by 30-40 mm. The 1 ton of additional weight of the new armament and armour caused performance to worsen.

In total, around 180 heavy Turán tanks were produced up to the end of 1944. The first 28 tanks were handed over to the armoured troops in July 1943. Training began only in the autumn of 1943. The Hungarians also designed a special command vehicle based on the Turán, the 43. M Turán signals/command vehicle. It had no turret armament, only a dummy gun barrel made of wood and a machine gun. The vehicle had a larger radio capacity and special stick radio antennas. The Ministry of Defence ordered 15 command vehicles, but it is likely that only the prototype was finished, in 1943.

Another invention was the 43. M long-barrelled heavy tank. The idea was to modify the original 75 mm short-barrelled gun to become more effective against the heavy Russian armour. The gun used was a L43 43. M 75mm, based on the German PAK 40. During test trials of the gun several problems arose, and allied air raids also created obstacles during the development, which was cancelled in the autumn of 1944.

Based on the current German practice and lessons learned at the front, in 1944 the medium and heavy Turáns received additional skirting plates, on the hull and on the turret. Some battle-damaged 40. M Turán tanks were rebuilt as 41. M models. The rearmament process, which involved the Turán 40 changing its turret to that of the Turán 75, was simple enough because the shape and radius of the two turrets were the same. The damaged turrets of the Turán 40 were simply replaced by Turán 75 turrets.

A command, signal version of the Turán was developed in 1944 on the basis of the H-802 vehicle , it accommodate enlarged signal capacity in return the main armament was a dummy one. [Éder Miklós]

41. M Turán heavy tank at the Armoured School, Esztergomtábor 1944. Behind the Turán the turret of the Lt. vz. 35 light tank visible. [Szollár János]

41. M Turán heavy tank on firing exercise, the new Turán heavy tanks just started to arrive to the tank battalions in late 1943. [Bonhardt Attila]

Technical Data

Designation: **40. M Turán I (Turán 40) medium tank**
Years of production: 1941-1943
Factory/ produced quantity: Weis Manfred Factory, MÁVAG, Ganz, Magyar Vaggon/ 285
Combat weight: 18.7 t
Length: 5530 mm
Width: 2444 mm
Height: 2355 mm
Ground pressure: 0,61 kp/cm/3,
Crew: 5
Engine: Weiss Manfred V-8 H 4
Displacement: 14866 cm/3
Cylinders: 8
Horsepower: 260 Hp
Speed: 47,2 km/h
Range: 165 km on road
Obstacles:
– step: 0,8 m
– ditch: 2,2 m
– ford: 0,9 m
Armament:
– one 41. M 40 mm gun
– range: 4500 m
– rate of fire: 12 rounds/minute
– two 34/40. AM 8 mm machine-guns
– crew self-protection weapons three 39. M submachine guns
Ammunition:
– 101 40 mm armour piercing and fragmentation shell
– 3000 8 mm machine gun cartridge
– 840 9 mm sub-machine gun cartridge
– 5 smoke candles
Armour: 13-50 mm
Radio: one R-5/a and one R-4 radio with stick antenna
Number plates:
– WM – H-803 - H-871
– MÁVAG – 1H-201 – 1H- 268
– MWG – 1H-001 – 1H-086
– Ganz – 1H-426 – 1H-489

Designation: **41M Turán II (Turán 75) heavy tank**
Years of production: 1943-1944
Factory/ produced quantity: Weis Manfred Factory, M. Vaggon, Ganz/ 129-189
Combat weight: 19,2 t (without skirt plates)

Lined up heavy tank company equipped with 41. M Turán heavy tanks. The tanks turrets covered with canvas protection against dust or rain. The tanks have three tones camouflage. [Bonhardt Attila]

Length: 5530 mm
Width: 2440 mm
Height: 2380 mm
Ground pressure: 0,64 kp/cm/3
Crew: 5
Engine: Weis Manfred V-8 H
Displacement: 14866 cm/3
Cylinders: 8
Horsepower: 260 Hp
Speed: 45 km/h
Range: 165 km on road
Obstacles:
– step: 0,80 m
– ditch: 2,2 m
– ford: 0.9 m
Armament:
– one 41. M 75 mm short barrel gun
– range: 6300 – 8400 m
– rate of fire: 12 shots/ minute
– two 34/40. AM 8 mm machine-guns
Crew self-protection weapons: three 9mm 39. M sub-machine gun
Ammunition:
– 56 75mm armoured piercing and fragmentation shell
– 3000 machine gun cartridge
– 840 9mm submachine cartridge
– 5 smoke candles
Armour: 13-50 mm
Radio: one R-5/a and one R-4 radio with stick antenna
Number plates:
– WM: 2H-000 – 2H-061, 2H-077 – 2H-086
– MWG: 2H-201 – 2H-235, 2H-436 – 2H-458, 1H-083
– Ganz: 2H-400 – 2H-435

Designation: **43. M Turán III (Turán 75 long barrelled) heavy tank**
Years of production: 1943-1944
Factory/produced quantity: Weis Manfred Factory/ one prototype
Combat weight: 23,3 t (with skirt plates)
Length: 6860 mm (with gun)
Width: 2650 mm (with skirt plates)
Height: 2650 mm
Ground pressure: 0,78 kp/cm/3
Crew: 4-5
Engine: Manfred Weiss V-8 H
Displacement: 14866 cm/3
Cylinders: 8
Horsepower: 260 Hp
Speed: 37 km/h (with skirt plates)

Range: 165 km on road
Obstacle – step: 0,8 m
– ditch: 2,2 m
– ford: 0,9 m
Armament: one 43. M L55 75 mm gun
range: 7500 – 8600 m
rate of fire: 12 shots/minute
two 34/40. AM 8 mm machine-guns
Crew self-protection weapons: three 9 mm 39. M sub-machine gun
Ammunition:
– 32 75mm armoured piercing and fragmentation shell
– 3000 8 mm machine gun cartridge
– 840 9 mm sub-machine gun cartridge
– 5 smoke candles
Armour: 13-75 mm
Radio: one R-5/a and one R-4 radio with stick antenna
Number plates: H-830 prototype

40/43. M Zrínyi Assault Howitzer

The most successful Hungarian armoured vehicle of WWII was the Zrínyi assault gun. It was entirely designed from parts of the Turán (chassis) and 60 gun barrels left over from Turán production were also incorporated in the Zrínyis.

Although a stop-gap measure, it proved to be very effective. German experiences on the front had shown the need for the Hungarian armoured forces to have an assault gun, but German inflexibility meant that Hungary could not purchase German weapons.

The General Staff had decided to equip the artillery units of the armoured divisions with assault guns and howitzers in 1942. This decision coincided with the idea by the Manfred Weiss Company to develop a vehicle that was more powerful than the heavy Turán.

According to unconfirmed sources, Hungarian experts visited Italy somewhere 1941-42, where they were shown around the factory where Semovente assault guns were produced for the Italian Army. The Italian Semovente self-propelled gun was designed on the basis of the Italian M13/40 medium tank in 1941. There is no proofed evidence whether the Hungarians were influenced by their Italian colleges. At least we can say that the concept of the Italian and Hungarian design was very similar.

The Turán chassis was selected as the basis for the assault gun, and the gun chosen was the 40. M 105mm howitzer. This seemed to be the fastest and least expensive solution. In 1942 the first iron prototype was produced, registration number H801.

The wooden bridge collapsed under the weight of a 40/43. M Zrínyi assault howitzer belonged to the 1. Assault gun Battalion, in the Carpathian Mountain. The Zrínyi carries fuel drums, the hatches are open the crew leaved the vehicles to bring help to extract their precious beast. [Mujzer Péter]

Destroyed 40/43. M Zrínyi assault howitzer left on the battlefield, at Kelenföld, Budapest in summer of 1945. Probably an internal explosion caused the death of the assault howitzer. [Bonhardt Attila]

On the summer of 1945, an abandoned Zrínyi belonged to 1. Lt Tibor Rácz, 1/3. Assault Gun Battery, rest in a temporarily junk yard at Vérmező, Budapest. 1. Lt Rácz was captured at the end of the siege. He tried to escape but was shot. He died later on due to his wound. [Fortepan 45609]

Withdrawing troops of the 2. Battery 1. Assault Gun Battalion at the Carpathian Mountains, summer of 1944. Behind the Zrínyi assault howitzer is a 38. M Botond truck. The tactical numbering 2+2, means 2. vehicles of the battery. [Bonhardt Attila]

Resting crew and the 40/43. M Zrínyi assault howitzer belong to the 1/3 Battery, during the lull of the fighting at Stanislau, River Bystricza. The hull of the Zrínyi reinforced with spare tracks. [Bonhardt Attila]

The crew of the 40/43. M Zrínyi assault howitzer at Hajmáskér firing range wait for instruction, the low shape of the assault howitzer is evident. [Bonhardt Attila]

The turret was removed, and the howitzer was mounted in the hull. The new weapon was designated the 40/43. M Zrínyi assault howitzer. The assault gun underwent test trials in Hajmáskér in the winter of 1942/43.

The Ministry of Defence ordered 40 assault howitzers in January 1943. The fighting ability of the Turán could not be improved so the plan was to mass produce the assault howitzers. In order to combat the fighting skills of the Russian T-34 tank, it was decided to produce an assault gun with a 75 mm gun on the same chassis, named the Zrínyi I assault gun.

The plan was to organise an assault gun battalion for each infantry and cavalry division. The first assault gun battalions were set up and equipped with 34 Zrínyis in March 1944, but 40/43. M Zrínyi production was slow.

The Zrínyi I prototype was finished in February 1944, but the long barrelled gun had some problems which were not possible to solve. Only the prototype of the assault gun was finished. On July 27, 1944 an allied air raid hit and severely damaged the Manfred Weiss factory, which ended mass production; about 15- 20 half-finished Zrínyis and other parts were recovered from under the wreckage. The last Zrínyis were produced at

Side view of the abandoned 40/43. M Zrínyi assault howitzer belonged to 1. Lt Tibor Rácz, 1/3. Assault Gun Battery, rest in a temporarily junk yard at Vérmező. Behind the Zrínyi the destruction of the city seen, the demolished and burned out buildings. [Bonhardt Attila]

the Ganz factory during the siege of Budapest. The last known registration number was H066, but it cannot be confirmed whether the troops received the last 20-22 Zrínyis. According to different sources, between 40 and 66 Zrínyis were produced. During the siege of Budapest six assembled Zrínyis from the Ganz factory went directly to the front line.

40/43. M Zrínyi assault howitzer belongs to the 2. Battery of the 10. Assault Gun Battalion waits in an ambush position at 22 September 1944, Torda. [Bonhardt Attila]

40/43. M Zrínyi assault howitzer and its 4 men crew, belonged to the 1. Battery of the 1. Assault gun Battalion, summer 1944 Galicia. The front and the side of the hull reinforced with spare tracks and skirt plates. [Szollár János]

40/43. M Zrínyi assault howitzer belonged to the 1. Battery of the 1. Assault Gun Battalion, the unit sign skull with crossed guns, painted on the mudguard, whit 1 means 1. Battery. [Szollár János]

The HTI made efforts to reinforce the firepower of the Zrínyi assault howitzers using the German Nebelwerfer rocket launchers in late 1943, early 1944. The original Nebelwerfer rocket launcher had six 15cm rocket tubes already used by the Hungarian Army, it was divided to two packs of three rocket tubes and were attached to each rear side of the hull. The concept was to use the rocket fire to annihilate the enemy anti-tank position in time before the Zrínyis reach the killing zone of the anti-tank gun. The practical range of the rockets were about 2000-7000 meter. In theory a fire strike of 6 15 cm Nebelwerfer rockets could destroy a whole anti-tank battery by hitting the identified position of the enemy. Except the experimental vehicle

Technical Data

Designation: **40/43. M Zrínyi (Zrínyi 105) assault howitzer**
Years of production: 1942-1944
Factory/produces quantity: Weis Manfred Factory/ 66+ 6(?)
Combat weight: 21,50 t – 22,5 t with skirt plates
Length: 5900 mm (with gun)
Width: 2890 mm
Height: 1900 mm
Ground pressure: 0,75 kp/cm/3
Crew: 4
Engine: Manfred Weiss V8
Displacement: 14866 cm/3

Zrínyi assault howitzer belonged to the 1. Battery (3. vehicle) 1. Assault Gun Battalion, the assault howitzer has the side skirt plates with large military insignia and tactical numbers. [Szollár János]

The iron prototype of the 40/43. M Zrínyi assault howitzer at Hajmáskér on evaluation course, this iron prototype was also the test vehicle for the assault gun version of the Zrínyi armed with long barrelled 7.5cm gun. [Éder Miklós]

The 3H-001, Zrínyi assault howitzer, next to the vehicle is Lt. Rácz Tibor. He lead into the firing position of his vehicle on a live firing exercise at hajmáskér. [Éder Miklós]

Cylinders: 8
Horsepower: 260 Hp
Speed: 43 km/h – 40 km/h with skirt plates
Range: 220 km on road
Obstacles:
– steps: 0,8 m
– ditch: 2,2 m
– ford: 0,9 m
Armament:
– one 40. M 105 mm L/20 howitzer
range: 10,500 m
rate of fire: 6 shots/minute
Ammunition: 52 105mm shell, 30 fragmentation, 16 armoured piercing and 6 smoke
Armour: 13-75 mm
Radio: one R-5/a radio with stick antenna

Designation: 44. M Zrínyi (Zrínyi 75) assault gun
Years of production: 1944
Factory/produced quantity: Weis Manfred Factory/ one prototype

Combat weight: 22 t
Length: 7350 mm with gun
Width: 2890 mm
Height: 1900 mm
Ground pressure: 0,72 kp/cm/3
Crew: 4
Engine: Manfred Weiss V8-4
Displacement: 14866 cm
Cylinders: 8
Horsepower: 260 Hp
Speed: 43km/h - 40 km/h with skirt plates
Range: 220 km on road
Obstacle:
– step: 0,8 m
– ditch: 2,2 m
– ford: 0,9 m
Armament: one 43. M 75 mm L55 gun
rate of fire: 12 rounds/minute
Armour: 13-75 mm
Radio: one R-5/a radio with stick antenna

Resting crew on the top of the 40/43. M Zrínyi assault howitzer, the 8/14. M artillery sight used for indirect firing is visible on the top of the vehicle, between the sitting crew. [Bonhardt Attila]

Rear view of a 40/43. M Zrínyi assault howitzer on the street of Vác late 1944. Between the metal box and the spare wheel are the smoke candles. [Karai Sándor]

40/43. M Zrínyi assault howitzer ready to move, the commander, Lt. Tibor Rátz and the gunner, Lt. László Csengeri Pap sitting in the open hatches wears the 37. M crash helmet. [Bonhardt Attila]

Sunbathing crew of the 3H-001, Zrínyi assault howitzer belongs to the 1/2. Battery at Hajmáskér on training exercise in 1943. [Bonhardt Attila]

Experimental Heavy Tank and Assault Gun
44. M Tas Heavy Tank

In 1943 the Hungarian General Staff, faced with the impossibility of purchasing such a tank from the Germans, took the decision to design a true heavy tank for the armoured troops. The project was named Tas and assigned to the Manfred Weiss factory. The plan was to build a tank that resembled the shape of the German Panther. The main armament of the Tas was one 75 mm or 80 mm long barrelled gun. The prototype was completed in March 1944, but continued allied air raids and the lack of materials forced the project to be cancelled.

Another experimental vehicle was the Tas assault gun which also was designed by Manfred Weiss in 1944. It had a very favourable low silhouette, similar to the Zrínyi, and with a powerful German gun. Again due to the constant allied air raids and the lack of materials this project was also cancelled.

Rear view of the 40/43. M Zrínyi assault howitzer, rear door is open, the rear door was kept open in action too, to provide ventilation and the empty shell cases ejected through it. [Bonhardt Attila]

Technical Data

Designation: **44. M Tas heavy tank**
Years of production: 1944
Combat weight: 36 t
Length: 6300 mm without gun
Width: 3150 mm
Height: 2520 mm
Ground pressure: 0,7 kp/cm/3
Crew: 5
Engine: two Manfred Weiss V8H-4
Displacement: 2 x 14866 cm/3
Cylinders: 8
Horsepower: 520 Hp
Speed: 45 km/h
Range: 200 km
Obstacle:
– step: unknown
– ditch: unknown
– ford: unknown
Armament:
– one KwK 75 mm L46 gun
– two 34/40A M 8 mm machine-guns
Ammunition:
Armour: 20-120 mm
Radio: R-5/a

Armoured Cars

The Hungarian military was interested in using armoured cars from the very beginning but again it proved difficult to

purchase or produce a modern version. In 1933 Mike Straussler, a former Hungarian engineer, designed a new four-wheel drive armoured car for the British Army and asked the Manfred Weiss factory to produce the prototype for him. The AC I was manufactured in 1934.

The Hungarian Army recognised the advantages of the vehicle but lacked the money to purchase it. Manfred Weiss and engineer Straussler developed a new vehicle in 1935. The AC II was a true military armoured car with one front and one rear driving seat, and compartments, which were important on a reconnaissance mission.

The Weiss Company produced two prototypes, one of which was for the British Army. The other remained at the factory, and with the guidance of the HTI a turret was designed for it. At that time the Hungarians also tested the ADKZ, Daimler-Benz, and A-S-P armoured cars.

In 1938 MAVAG got the plans for the Swedish Lynx armoured car. The HTI gave permission to the factory to purchase and test one.

39. M Csaba Armoured Car

After the successful trials with the AC II, in 1939 the Ministry of Defence ordered this model designated the Csaba, for the reconnaissance units. The hull and turret of the vehicle were designed jointly by Manfred Weiss and the HTI. It had an ideal shape, the armour plating being situated obliquely on the vehicle for added protection against bullets. The vehicle had one 20mm anti-tank rifle and one 8mm machine-gun in the front of

Vehicles maintenance of an armoured car platoon in a stream somewhere in Ukraine, the closest 39. M Csaba number plate Pc.114, the number plates still painted on a white background. The photo was taken by 2. Lt. Imre Suhay, he was killed in action the next year at River Don with the 30. Tank Regiment. [Mujzer Péter]

Photo taken by 1. Lt. Béla Király, "towards to Donetsk in mud and water". The motorised rifle brigades reached this area in October 1941. The Ford-Marmon truck tows an ex-Polish fuel trailer. Next to them is a 39. M Csaba armoured car. [Mujzer Péter]

Csaba Armoured Car Company belongs to the 1. Armoured Cavalry Battalion moves forward on the muddy road in Voivodina, April of 1941. A bundle of logs were attached to the armoured car to negotiate the muddy terrain. [Móker József]

39. M Csaba armoured car, number plate Pc.124 belonged to the 1. Reconnaissance Battalion at a checkpoint on Romanian-Hungarian border in September 1940, in front of the armoured car a 37mm 36. M anti-tank gun. [Fortepan 15602]

The forward driver station of the 39. M Csaba armoured, above the driver seat the weapons mountings visible. [Fortepan 4390]

Armoured cars assemble at the yard of the Automobile Depot, in the centre is a 39. M Csaba armoured car, on the left is the Strausler ACII without armament. [Fortepan 72133, Lissák Tivadar]

the turret, and one 8mm light machinegun was located to fire through the open rear turret hatch as an anti-aircraft weapon. In 1939 the Ministry of Defence ordered 61 x 39M Csabas and a further 20 x 39M and 12 x 40M command vehicles were ordered and delivered by Manfred Weiss in 1940. It appears that there was a third order for about 70 armoured cars, but there is no confirmation as to whether these were made and delivered.

40. M Csaba Armoured Command Car

The Army also ordered special command vehicles, the Csaba 40. M, for the reconnaissance units, which had a greater radio capacity. The main requirement for this model was for it to be very similar to the combat vehicle, in order to keep

Internal photo of the turret of the 39. M Csaba armoured car, the 34/37. M 8mm machine gun is on the right. [Fortepan 43905]

The prototype of the Csaba armoured car was the ACII Strausler armoured car, it used for training at the Ludovika Academy. [Fortepan 43910]

Cadets of the Ludovika Academy are on a driving exercise with 39. M Csaba armoured car. The cadets wear two pieces leather protective suits. [Fortepan 43934]

39. M Csaba armoured car belongs to the Armoured Car Platoon of the 1. Mountain Brigade, summer of 1941, Carpathian Mountains, the white 1.hgy. is the unit sign, stands for the 1. Mountain Brigade. [Mujzer Péter]

39. M Csaba armoured car company wait for marching orders, in front of the armoured cars is a Mercedes G5 staff car, April 1941. The armoured cars and the staff car painted in same three tones camouflage. [Deák Tamás]

40. M Csaba armoured command/signal car passing the advancing German infantry during the operation in Ukraine in summer of 1941. The antenna frame of the signal car is in elevated position ready for transmitting. [Mujzer Péter]

40. M Csaba armoured command/signal car with elevated antenna frame. The number plates for the 40. M Csaba strated with Pc.400. [Bonhardt Attila]

production simple and so as to avoid drawing special enemy attention to it. The command vehicle received a smaller turret with only one 8mm machine-gun, and a special lattice radio mast.

Only a dozen were built officially, though it is likely that a few damaged 39. M were converted to command vehicles during the war. In March 1943, 50 modified Csabas, designated Hunor, were requested from the Manfred Weiss factory. There is no information available whether any Hunor armoured cars were delivered.

Technical Data

Designation: **39. M Csaba armoured car**
Years of production: 1939 – 1943
Factory/ produced quantity: Weis Manfred Factory/ 97
Combat weight: 6.4 t
Length: 4520 mm
Width: 2100 mm
Height: 2370 mm
Ground pressure:
Crew: 4
Engine: Ford
Displacement: 3560 cm/3
Cylinders: 8
Horsepower: 90-95 Hp
Speed: 65 km/h

Range: 150-200 km
Obstacle:
– step: 0,5 m
– ditch: 0,5 m
– ford: 1 m
Armament:
– 36. M 20 mm anti-tank rifle;
– 34/37. AM 8 mm machine-gun;
– 31. M 8 mm light machine-gun
Ammunition:
– 200 20mm shell
– 3000 8 mm machinegun cartridge
Armour: 9-13 mm
Radio: R-4 with frame and stick antenna

Designation: **40. M Csaba command car**
Years of production: 1940 -1943
Factory/produced quantity: Weis Manfred Factory/ 20+2
Combat weight: 6.2 t
Length: 4520 mm
Width: 2100 mm
Height: 2300 mm
Ground pressure:
Crew: 4
Engine: Ford
Displacement: 3560 cm/3

39. M Csaba armoured car belongs to the 1. Reconnaissance Battalion advancing in the Mountains of Carpathian in summer of 1941, the vehicles painted in three tones camouflage, octagonal military insignia and white lightning bolt unit sign. [Mujzer Péter]

Cylinders: 8
Horsepower: 90-95 Hp
Speed: 70 km/h
Range: 150-200 km
Obstacle:
– step: 0,5 m
– ditch: 0,5
– ford: 1 m
Armament: 34/37. AM 8 mm machine-gun
Ammunition: 4000 8 mm machine gun cartridges
Armour: 9-13 mm
Radio: one R-4T, two R-4 with frame antenna

Ammunition Rates of the Armoured Forces Vehicles

The following shows the official ammunition carrying capacity of the vehicles:
38. M Toldi I-II: 208 x 20 mm and 2400 x 8 mm
38. M Toldi IIA: 55 x 40 mm and 3200 x 8 mm
38. M Toldi III: 87 x 40 mm 3200 x 8 mm
40. M Nimród: 160 x 40 mm
40. M Turán: 101 x 40 mm and 3000 x 8 mm
41. M Turán: 52 x 75 mm and 3000 x 8 mm
43. M Turán: 32 x 75 mm and 1800 x 8 mm or 52 x 75 mm and 3000 x 8 mm
40/43 Zrínyi: 52 x 105 mm (in action they carried 90-95 x 105 mm shell

Vehicle Costs

During production there was an ongoing discussion between the Ministry of Defence and the factories about the prices to be charged for each vehicle. In reality, the price actually paid by the Ministry was a compromise; more or less half-way between the prices asked for by the factories and the offer prices from the Ministry. Note: The exchange rate in 1936 was US$1 = 3.40 Pengő.

Type	Factory price	Price offered by the army
Turán 40	290,000 pengo	245,000 Pengs
Turán 75	325,000-	280,000
Nimród	175,000-	141,000
Toldi	190,000-	151,000
Csaba	112,000-	93,000

Production of Armoured Vehicles

	M. Weiss	Ganz	Rába (1)	MAVAG	Total
Toldi		108 (2)		82	190
Turán I	70	74	82	59	285
Turán II	54	36	55		145
Zrínyi	40+14				40+14
Csaba	93				93
Nimród				135	135

(1) The Rába Factory was officially named Magyar Vagon és Gépgyár and situated at Győr
(2) Ganz modified 80 Toldi IIA with the 40 mm gun, and converted 9 medical Toldis.

Official Vehicle Designations

The Hungarian-made armoured vehicles had different designations during their use. There were one or more official designations, and of course the troops used their own common names. The names shown in parentheses were official designations used in the later part of the war.

Crew of the armoured car, officers and enlisted men stands in front of a 39. M Csaba armoured car, painted in dark olive green camouflage with small size military insignia. [Szollár János]

Armoured car company of the 1. Reconnaissance Battalion lined up for inspection, the 39. M Csaba armoured cars have three tones camouflage and Maltese cross military insignia on the turret and the hull. [Szollár János]

38M Toldi light tank - 1st order (Toldi A20)
38. M Toldi light tank - 2nd order (Toldi B20)
38. M Toldi IIA light tank (Toldi B40)
38. M Toldi III light tank (Toldi C40)
43. M Toldi medical tank (Toldi EU20)
40. M Nimród self-propelled AA/AT gun
43. M Lehel troop/medical carrier
40. M Turán medium tank (Turán 40) or Turán I
41. M Turán heavy tank (Turán75 short-barrelled) or Turán II
43. M Turán command tank
43. M Turán heavy tank (Turán75 long-barrelled)
40/43. M Zrínyi assault howitzer (Zrínyi 105) or Zrínyi II
44. M Zrínyi assault gun (Zrínyi 75) or Zrínyi I

CHAPTER VII

Foreign Armoured Vehicles in Hungarian service

The Hungarian Army used a lot of foreign armoured vehicles during the WWII. Some of these were purchased by the Hungarian military, while others were handed over by the Germans at the front. These latter vehicles remained in German service but were crewed by Hungarians under Hungarian tactical command. Additional vehicles that had been abandoned by the Germans were recovered and used by the Hungarians.

Dark blue police 39. M Csaba armoured cars with police sidecar motorcycles wait at the Vajdahunyad Cassel, Budapest 1944. [Pálinkás Zsolt]

LK-II light tank

In 1920 Hungary was able to purchase 14 LK tanks from Sweden. These were concealed in depots until 1927, but at that time only 5-7 remained serviceable. The unusable tanks were removed from the order of battle and the hulls were used for firing exercises and later sold as scrap.

FIAT 3000 B light tank

In 1930, five FIAT tanks were ordered secretly without armament; the troops used them for training equipped only with a machine-gun. In 1942 these were removed from the order of battle and used as targets for artillery.

35. M Fiat Ansaldo tankette

The Hungarian military purchased 150 CV-35 tankettes from Italy and named them the 35. M Ansaldo. They also received one CV-33 (H-169), and a flame-thrower tankette (H-164) which provided by the Italian for trials and testing. It remained in Hungary without any official purchase contract. The armament of the Ansaldo was modified to one twin 34M 8mm Gebauer machine-gun.

The Hungarians modified the observer cupola, which was put above the machine gunner's seat; each platoon commander's vehicle had this cupola installed. The HTI examined the possibilities of installing a turret with 360 degrees traverse but the project was cancelled due to the extra weight that this would add to the vehicle. In 1942 the surviving Ansaldos were handed over to the Hungarian Police and Gendarmerie, and 10 were delivered to the Croatian forces.

TKS tankette

After Germany's 1939 Polish Campaign, 15-20 TKS tankettes from the 10th Polish Cavalry Brigade escaped to Hungary. After intensive maintenance, which was carried out by interned Polish tank crews, the tankettes were handed over to the mobile troops for use in training. One TKS was later located in Zenta as a training vehicle, where it was captured by Yugoslavian partisans in 1944. This tankette is now exhibited in Belgrade.

R-35 light tank

Three Polish R-35 light tanks arrived in Hungary in the same way as the TKS. The 1st Reconnaissance Battalion also used these for training. One of the vehicles was captured by the Red Army at Budapest in 1945.

Hotchkiss H-35 and H-39 light tanks

In 1942 Hungarian forces carried out security operations behind the front lines in the Ukraine. To carry out this mission the 101st Independent Light Tank Company was formed, and equipped by the Germans with 15 Hotchkiss light tanks. The unit fought against partisans until March 1943 when the remaining 6 tanks were destroyed by advancing Russian regular forces.

SOUMA S-35 medium tank

The 101st Independent Light Tank Company also received two S-35 tanks as command vehicles for use in operations against partisans in the Ukraine. Most likely these were also destroyed during the operations.

T-27 tankette

The Hungarian troops captured a few serviceable Russian T-27 tankettes in the Ukraine, which were used as tractors on the front. These were transported back to Hungary and used for training.

T-11 (Lt-35) light tank

In 1939, during the occupation of Carpathian-Ukraine, the advancing Hungarian troops captured two damaged Lt-35 light tanks. They were later repaired by the Skoda Company and used by the Armour Training Centre at Esztergomtábor.

Skoda 38(t) light tank

The Hungarians received from the Germans 108 Skoda 38(t) G light tanks in the spring of 1942 to equip the 1st Armoured Field Division. Among the 38(t) were 38 command and 70 normal vehicles, the only differences between the two being the radio instruments. In 1943 the surviving nine Skodas were handed over to the 1st Cavalry Division to be used in training

Pz.Kpfw. I B (Sd.Kfz. 101)

In 1937 Hungary purchased one Pz.Kpfw. I for testing, although it was already an outdated model at that time. The vehicle was later used for training purposes. The 1st Armoured Field Division received 8 Pz.Kpfw. I for training, among which was a Pz.Kpfw. IA which later was reassigned to the 1st Cavalry Division.

Pz.Kpfw. I B (Sd.Kfz. 265)

The 1st Armoured Field Division received 6 armoured command vehicles on the front in 1942; there is no further information about these.

Pz.Kpfw. II F

The Germans planned to equip the light platoons of the 1st Armoured Field Division with Pz.Kpfw.II, but for lack of available vehicles the plan was cancelled. However, a few were assigned to the Hungarians for training at the front. It appears that the 3/II Tank Battalion also had two vehicles in 1944.

7.5 cm Pak 40/2 auf Gw.II. Marder II Tank Hunter

The 1st Armoured Field Division were loaned 5 Marders by the Germans for use at the front, but after completing their mission the surviving tank hunters were sent back to Germany in 1943.

Pz.Kpfw. III M

At the front the 1st Armoured Field Division received 10 Pz.Kpfw. III M with L/60 50mm guns and German crews to compensate for casualties suffered by the division. In 1943 the HTI had one Pz.Kpfw. III M. for testing but by 1943 it was already outdated. The 2nd Armoured Division had 10-12 Pz.Kpfw. III M tanks in the summer of 1944.

Pz.Kpfw. IV F 1

The 1st Armoured Field Division was equipped with 22 Pz.Kpfw. IV F 1 in 1942. Only one survived the winter offensive.

Pz.Kpfw. IV F2

To compensate for losses suffered by the 1st Armoured Field Division, it received 10 F2 on loan at the front in the autumn of 1942. The one surviving tank was returned to the Germans in 1943.

Pz.Kpfw. IV H

The 30th Tank Regiment was equipped with 12 Pz.Kpfw. IV H tanks. In late 1944 additional tanks were handed over to the Hungarian Army. Between 1944/45, the total received by the Hungarian armoured forces was in the region of 72.

Pz.Kpfw. V Panther

In the summer of 1944 the Hungarian Army wanted to enlarge the strength of its armoured divisions with one Pz.Kpfw. IV and one Pz.Kpfw. V tank battalion. In accordance with this plan five Panthers were handed over to the troops in August to be used for training. After Romania's change of sides, 10-12 Panthers originally destined for Romania were donated to Hungary and used in the fighting in Transylvania in 1944.

Pz.Kpfw. VI E Tiger

The first Tigers were given to the Hungarian troops during the advance in Galicia in 1944. The 3rd Tank Regiment received 10 Tigers to replace knocked out Turáns, and a further three were later presented as a birthday present to Major-General László Hollós-Kuthy. In the spring of 1945 another Hungarian company fought with German-marked Tigers.

StuG III G Assault Gun

In 1942 a German unit of 10 StuG III was temporarily subordinated to the 1st Armoured Field Division. In June 1944, the 2nd Armoured Division's losses were compensated for with 10 long-barrelled (L/48) StuG III G. assault guns in Galicia. The Hungarian military also received 40 StuG III G assault guns which were used to equip the 7th Assault Gun Battalion in August 1944.

Jagdpanzer 38. (t) Hetzer

According to unconfirmed German sources, the Hungarians received about 130 Hetzers between October 1944 and January 1945. The Hetzers were used by the assault gun crews who had no Zrínyis. The 20th Assault Gun Battalion had 15 Hetzers in March 1945.

Conclusion

During the WWII, the leading Axis and Allied powers produced armoured vehicles in enormous quantity. Germany built 43000 tanks and assault guns. Soviet Union produced 87000 tanks and 25000 assault guns.

The Hungarian war industry produced 916 (plus 57 unconfirmed) armoured vehicles. During the war, the Hungarian Army also got 623 (plus 115 unconfirmed) foreign armoured vehicles. These vehicles were originated from the next countries; 158 from Italy, 396 (plus106) from Germany, 2 from Sweden, 4 from Czechoslovakia, 18 (plus 7) from France, 16 from Poland, 4 from UK, 22 from Su and 3 (plus 2) from USA.

All in all 1539 (plus 172 unconfirmed) armoured vehicles served under the Hungarian flag during the WWII. This quantity and quality did not match with the German, Italian numbers; do not even mention the Soviet production.

On the other hand we have to note the Hungarian war industry was the fourth largest among the Axis. Against all odds and restrictions of the Peace Treaty and the weak financial state of the country, Hungary was able to develop a significant heavy war industry. This industry was able to produce vehicles under license, modified and upgraded existing vehicles and developed home designed ones.

Rear number plate, Pc.146 of the 39. M Csaba armoured car painted on a white square and a small size octagonal military insignia. [Fortepan 43909]

Comparing with our neighbours, especially with Romania, which was a sworn enemy of Hungary, the numbers are striking. The Romanian Army possessed with 1051 foreign armoured vehicles during the war. Just 126 French UE armoured, tracked vehicles were assembled in Romania.

The Slovakian Army had 234, the Bulgarian Army had 346 and the Finnish Army had 598 armoured vehicles during the war.

CHAPTER VIII

Camouflage and markings

Camouflage

Initially, the armoured and motor vehicles had no standard camouflage; up to the end of the 1930s each type had a different colour. The vehicles of the RUISK were painted dark blue to symbolize that these were on police duty. The Vickers armoured cars were dark blue up to 1936, but were then repainted olive green. The wheeled vehicles were olive green in colour in the beginning. Later the military vehicles were painted with three-tone standard camouflage. The mobilised civilian trucks wore their original paint.

The LK and Fiat tanks had a three-tone camouflage, with the basic colours being khaki, olive-green, yellow. The Ansaldo tankettes arrived with Italian-style colours, with a basic colour of light sand/yellow in 1937. The Hungarian armoured vehicles manufactured from 1940 were finished in French-style camouflage consisting of a base colour of dark olive green with light ochre and red-brown blotches.

Until 1942, this disruptive camouflage was brush-applied with hard-edged patterns of irregular blotches. However, in 1942 the Hungarians began to use spray equipment on the Turáns and other types, giving the camouflage patterns a more diaphanous appearance. In 1944, some of the armoured and non-armoured vehicles were uniformly painted dark green. At least one Csaba platoon belonged to the 2nd Reconnaissance Battalion was painted and delivered to the Eastern front in light ochre in 1944.

Also in 1944, two or five 39 M Csaba armoured cars were handed over to the mobile reserve of the State Police. The known two Csabas, RR-711 and 712 were painted dark blue.

An army regulation defined the camouflage colours to be used, but the style of the patches varied according to the different factories where the vehicles were produced.

The foreign-supplied equipment was generally used in its original colours. The German equipment of the 1st Armoured Field Division was in panzer grey, and the Tigers had their distinctive three-tone camouflage. The German vehicles which were handed over at the front carried their own original colours, markings, numbers and even personal markings there being no time to make any changes.

National Military Insignia

The first insignia to appear on armour was that on the Romfell k. und k. armoured cars manned by Hungarian crews, during WWI. There was no separate Hungarian national insignia, thus the vehicles sported the black stemmed- or Maltese cross on a white quadrant of the monarchy's air force ("A"). The insignia was painted on both sides and on the armoured louvers on the front. The first change was made in 1919.

During the organisation of the new National Army the insurgents in Western-Hungary used two Bussing-Fross armoured cars having a white patriarchal cross ("B") painted over the base-coat on the front side-panels. Between 1919 and 1920 these vehicles were used by the Pronay detachment with unaltered insignia. In accordance with the 1920 peace-treaty limitations the armoured cars were decommissioned from the army but were retained in the security forces as so-called sentry-car and the insignia were removed.

The first proper, yet unofficial national insignia appeared on the armoured train no.102 during the 1938 campaign in Slovakia. The commander of the train got on his own initiative, the triangular red white-green air force insignia ("C") painted on both sides of the gun-wagon, with the tip facing up. After reaching the occupied destination the "selfish" insignia has to be over-painted upon order form high command. Change of policy was brought about in 1940 when Section 31b. of the Ministry of Defence on the 16th of July ordered armoured units to prepare proposals and designs for a unitary armour insignia. Every unit - the two armoured-reconnaissance and the two armoured cavalry battalions - designed and applied to the vehicles their own insignia.

The 1st Reconnaissance Battalion used a white Maltese cross ("D") as a base. The green or red outlines and the circle ("E,F,G") were to be painted in different combinations for each company

Unit sign of the 51. Sp. AT/AA Battalion painted on the back of the 40. M Nimród armoured vehicle, next to the unit sign is the number plate, the white square was left out from the number plate in 1942. [Fortepan 43957]

of the battalion (tankette, light-tank, armoured car). The insignia were painted on all four sides and, for aerial identification, onto the engine deck too. The Toldi tanks and the Csaba armoured cars had the insignia painted onto the turret sides while on the Ansaldos it was placed on the hull sides. The insignia was not applied on the rear hull of the Ansaldos. The insignia was painted on all battalion vehicles and was sported during the Transylvanian, Yugoslavian and Ukrainian campaigns. Nevertheless the design was rejected for the sake of "the national insignia must have an univocal and definite meaning" principle.

The vehicles of the 2nd Reconnaissance Battalion had a green cross ("H") outlined in white over a red circular base painted on five places. The Toldi tanks of the unit had the fifth insignia

38. M Toldi light tank with the temporarily unit sign of Filed Armoured Battalion based on the different armoured units of the Mobile Corps in summer of 1941. The whit triangle and the tulip painted on the turret of the tank. [Mujzer Péter]

on the top of the turret-hatch. This proposal was also rejected, but being similar to the accepted final octagonal insignia, the 2nd Reconnaissance Battalion was allowed to use it up to the end of 1941.

The Mechanised Forces Training- and Instruction-Camp Command suggested the use of a black Maltese cross ("I"). The proposal delineated the use of separate unit markings to distinguish the different sub-units. This proposal was also rejected by High Command.

The armoured battalion of the 2nd Cavalry Brigade proposed a white patriarchal cross outlined in red over a green, oval base ("J"). This insignia was painted only onto a single Toldi tank.

Finally Mobile Corps Command and the Institute of Military Technology jointly developed the octagonal insignia consisting of a green cross outlined in white and the area between the arms of the cross filled with red ("K").

The decision could be delayed no longer because of the imminent start of the Yugoslavian campaign in 1941. Thus following the Chief of Staff's order the last proposal was accepted as follows. The diameter of the insignia should be 500 mm, the green lines should be 80mm wide, and the white outline of the cross should be 50mm wide. The insignia should be painted onto the sides, front, rear and the top (engine deck) of vehicles. Whereas the insignia should not fit the intended location, the diameter should be modified to 350mm retaining the original proportions. The insignia in practice resulted to be too large and colourful. The insignia on the hull front, behind which sat the driver on Toldi tanks and Csaba armoured cars, made a perfect aiming-point for enemy anti-tank gunners (enough to think about the heavy white outlines of the cross). Therefore in the field crews often covered the front insignia with mud.

The order issued on the 16 of November 1942 prohibited the use of the old insignia and introduced a new, uniform one, already used by the air force - white cross over a black square ("L") - authorised in three different sizes according to the location on the vehicles. The instructions required the insignia to be placed on all visible sides of vehicles, but in practice it was applied only to the flanks and in increased size to the engine deck. Later of course there were occasions when the required dimensions of the insignia were visibly changed, e.g. on the Zrinyi assault-howitzers of the 1st Assault Artillery Battalion. Some reminiscences recall that on occasions only the white cross was applied without the black square. During the war several German vehicles were obtained either by purchase or by hand over. The 1st Armoured Field Division deployed in the Don area in 1942 had several Pz. IV. F1. and a great number of Skoda 38(t) tanks. These had the octagonal, tricolour 1941 type insig-

The non-armoured vehicles also wear their respective unit sign, this crashed KV-40 artillery tractor belonged to the II AA Battalion, 1. Armoured Division, the white rhombus was the unit sign of the 1. Armoured Division. [Fortepan 44081]

nia, while equipment handed over from 1943 on, retained the original German crosses in Hungarian service. The change of insignia was neglected mainly due to the shortages of time and material, but the original markings expressed perfectly the Axis affiliation. While never reached widespread use the national flag fixed over a frame to ease identification both from ground and air deserves mentioning. The size of the flag was 500x500 mm, increased, without the frame, to 1x1 m from 1944 on

Unit Insignia

The first unit signs were painted on the Ansaldos in 1938; these were white triangles on the training vehicles at Hajmáskér and Táborfalva. During the first mobilisation in 1938, the tankette companies were formed and assigned to the Mixed Brigades. Each unit invented its own colourful unit identification signs. Later, the standard requirements were to use adaptations of easy geometrical symbols, but these instructions did not yet exist when the early units were formed.

The regulations forbade the use of the Hungarian crown, wings or the death's head in a unit insignia. The crown was part of the national insignia, the air force used the wings, and the death's head belonged to the chemical warfare units. Nevertheless, almost all unit insignia incorporated at least one of these symbols.

In 1940, the High Command prohibited the use of any self-made signs on armoured vehicles. Only the 1st and 2nd Reconnaissance Battalions were authorised to use the 1 F (plus lightning bolt) and 2F markings on the vehicles.

In 1941 the Mobile Corps units used their own unit signs. However the deployed Tolids, Ansaldos of the armoured battalions also worn their original unit signs in the Ukrainian Campaign. According to the original photos we can find Toldi light tanks with lightning bolt, tank or skulk signs. Some cases the battalion sign was painted on the turret and the original unit sign were left on the hull.

There are some discrepancies with the unit signs of the motorised rifle battalions. Contrary to the official regulation for example the 3rd Motorised Rifle Battalion used three standing stripes instead of one horizontal stripe. The 4th Motorised Rifle Battalion used the white square instead of four leafs clover.

As of 1942 the units started to use the basic geometrical symbols, painted on the front and back mud-guards or the hull.

The Armoured Corps regulated the unit signs of the subordinated units in 1943. Interestingly not all of the units used the regulated unit signs. For example there is no decision in the regulation about the divisional signs for the armoured divisions. The 2nd Armoured Division used the white turned up triangle. According to the original photos, the 2nd Reconnaissance Battalion also used the white German eagle style unit sign instead of the authorised crossed swords in Galicia.

In 1944 the division and regiment (battalion) signs were painted on the left and right front and rear hull or mud-guards. The non-armoured vehicles also carried unit signs, following the above mentioned regulations.

The trucks of the armoured battalions carried the same unit signs as the armoured vehicles. The motorised rifle, artillery etc. troops invented their own unit signs during 1940-41. From 1942, all units of the 2nd Army, down to independent company level, were assigned unit signs. These signs were painted on the motor vehicles and horse-drawn carts.

License Plates

The Hungarian Army trucks and armoured vehicles also had a system of vehicle licence plates. The trucks had metal plates, while the armoured vehicles had painted licence plates. On the armoured vehicles, the front serial number was shown in a thin white rectangle. The style was usually an H, with the national shield (red-white-green), followed by a three digit serial number. The capital H referred to the Honvéd (Hungarian Army). The H and the numbers were painted in black. The same serial numbers were on the rear of the hull, but in a square shape.

Later, from 1944, the front license plate was simply painted on the camouflage without the white rectangle. On each license plate, the numbers identified the type of vehicle: 1 H identified the Turán 40M, 2H was the Turán 41M, and 3H was the Zrínyi.

Military trucks carried the same metal licence plates, also with the national shield, capital H and digits. Civilian trucks kept their civilian number plates.

Tactical Numbering

Hungarian armoured vehicles adopted the use of turret numbers in 1942. The 1st Armoured Field Division had large turret numbers. They were similar to the German-style three-digit identifications, and were used on both sides and back of the turret. They were painted only on the German supplied equipment, not on the Csabas and Toldis. During the final period prior to embarkation, they had experimental turret numbers done in different coloured chalk. Later they used the normal white painted numbers.

In 1944 the 2nd Armoured Division used a four-digit tactical number painted only on the rear plate of the turret. The Zrínyi assault gun battalions used different tactical numbers. Sometimes they showed the battalion and the battery number, e.g. 1+1, which meant the 1st Battery of the 1st Assault Gun Battalion, with the military insignia in the middle. In other cases, they indicated the battery number and the individual vehicle number, e.g. 2+2 or + 36.

Individual Markings

Individual markings were not typical among the Hungarian armoured troops. It was not regulated but was tolerated by the Army during the war. Even artillery pieces were named after fiancés and girlfriends according to contemporary film footages.

Nevertheless, at the end of the war some assault guns were found to have individual markings. The most well-known example was a knocked-out Zrínyi in Budapest, 1945, which after the siege was found with the inscription "SÁRI" visible on the observation port on the driver's side. The vehicle belonged to the 1/3rd Battery and was the personal vehicle of the battery commander, First Lieutenant Tibor Rátz.

CHAPTER IX

Colsing remarks

The end of the WWII found the fragmented remains of the Mobile Forces in Germany where the troops capitulated to the Allied Forces. Hungary lost the WWII as well as the WWI. It meant horrible losses and destruction to the country, to their citizens and to the Royal Hungarian Army.

38. M Toldi light tank in Ukraine, 1941, the tank had an original white skulk unit sign overpainted with white tulip unit sign. [Mujzer Péter]

The Hungarian Mobile Forces, as the whole Royal Hungarian Army, were prepared to carry out their main mission, the re-conquest of the lost territories of WWI from the Little Entente States. This goal was supported by the whole society, the political-military elite as well as the army.

The development of the Royal Hungarian Army and the Mobile Forces was carried out under difficult conditions, hampered by the harsh condition of the Peace Treaty of Trianon.

The Military leadership recognised the importance of modern mechanised warfare. The theoretical foundation and the organizational structure was laid down and carried out rather smoothly. However producing and maintaining the hardware was another issue.

Organising, arming and operating a modern mechanised force were an expensive business, even in peace time. Hungary opted for a mixed model, like most of the European States, it kept the traditional cavalry and cyclist formations augmented

German instructors and Hungarian trainees surround the Pz. VI-E Tiger tank, turret number 114, at Nadvorna summer of 1944. [Szollár János]

Broken dow Pz.VI-E Tiger tank in Galicia, summer of 1944. Hungarian junior officers stand at the tank, belonging to an infantry division's reconnaissance unit. [Szollár János]

Pz.IV.F tank belongs to the 30. Tank Regiment, 1. Armoured Field Division, at River Don, summer of 1942. [Deák Tamás]

Pz.VI.-E Tiger tank commanded by 1. Lt. Ervin Tarczay , belonged to 2. Company 3/I. Tank Battalion, turret number 214, summer of 1944. [Mujzer Péter]

Camouflaged StuG III, belonged to the 7. Assault Gun Battalion during the fighting in Hungary, authum of 1944. [Bonhardt Attila]

Pz.VI.-E Tiger tank, turret number 301, during the delayed, fighting retreat in Galicia, summer of 1944. [Mujzer Péter]

Hungarian Armored Forces in World War II

by the seeds of modern elements of armoured and motorised units. When the opportunity arose, the cyclist units were retrained as tank units.

By 1942 the Royal Hungarian Army had two armoured and one cavalry division. Compared to other minor Axis States, it was a remarkable achievement.

Hungary not only managed to organise its Mobile Forces but developed its war industry, which was capable of supplying the troops with home-designed armament and equipment. The Hungarian war industry was able to produce all kinds of weapons, armoured and non-armoured vehicles. However, the armoured vehicles made by the Hungarians were already outdated when they arrived at the troops.

The Royal Hungarian Army was deployed in the Soviet Union and not against its neighbours.

The Hungarian Mobile Forces had to face one of the most formidable army of its time, the Red Army. The technical and tactical shortfalls were evident from the very first days of the operation. However, the troops did their best, against all odds. They entered combat with the knowledge that even the heaviest Hungarian-made tank had just a minimum chance to challenge the Soviet T-34, which was not very promising. The men still did it and suffered dearly. Their ordeal was not finished by the end of the war.

They became prisoners of war, the lucky ones in the camps controlled by the Western Forces. The least fortunate ones were captured by the Red Army and spent, especially the officers, three to ten years in Soviet prison camps. The mortality rate was high in the camps. Even returning to Hungary was not a celebration. Hungary was under the direct occupation and political influence of the Soviet Union. Being a soldier of the Royal Hungarian Army was a negative mark on the men.

Especially the members of the Officer Corps found it difficult to reintegrate into Hungary.

After the war a few of them were accepted into the new, so called Democratic Army. Most of them were demobilised, put into retirement. They were subjected to mock trials, lost their pension and had to accept underclass jobs. Even those who could continue their career in the Democratic, later Peoples' Army did not serve too long. They had to get used to training and organising the new style Army. When it was completed, the luckier ones were kicked out of the Army. The less fortunate ones were arrested for years; some of them were even executed by the Communist Regime.

In the Annex of this book I am aiming at introducing four highly decorated members of the Mobile Forces. Their life stories are typical. Out of the four, one was killed in action, two emigrated and one died in poverty in Hungary.

After the WWII, Hungary as well as the Hungarian Peoples' Army was redesigned alongside the Soviet Regime. The new Hungarian Armoured Troops were organised, equipped and trained according to Red Army manuals. The Hungarian military traditions and lessons learned from the WWII were neglected and put aside. Very few items were preserved for the future. The most complete collection of the Hungarian armoured vehicles is currently kept in Kubinka, Russia.

ANNEX 1

Hungarian tanks in Soviet service

This annex based on the book of Maksim Kolomiets – Ilia Mosanskij: Trofei v Krasnoj Armij 1941-1945, Frontovaja Illustracija 1999.

Contrary to general belief, the Red Army extensively used captured armaments, vehicles from the beginning of the war.

The captured war materials were not just utilised but were carefully tested and evaluated by the Red Army experts.

The Red Army Mechanised and Armoured Directorate organised a dedicated section to deal with the collection and evaluation of the war booty as early as the end of 1941.

Even repair facilities were dedicated to put and keep the captured foreign trucks and armoured vehicles in service. Among the factories was the no. 37 "Red Proletarian" Factory. In 1942 the factory repaired 3 Pz. II, 3 Pz.38(t) and 115 trucks. The "Red Proletarian" continued the conversion of captured enemy trucks for the agricultural sector until 1955.

From 1942-43 the captured armoured vehicles started to emerge in significant number at the units. The Red Army also provided technical manuals to the troops and organised units to deploy the war booties. The previously Axis armoured vehicles were organised into independent companies, battalions or were subordinated directly to the Red Army tank units.

The enemy equipment was operated until they ran out of ammunition and spare parts. Of course the battlefields provided ample opportunity to replace the missing parts and ammunition. However, according to information available, the Russian crew was more confident with their homemade tanks.

The former enemy equipment had a significant shortfall: identification. In case of a combat situation, knowing who your friend is and who your enemy means death or life. The re-enlisted armoured vehicles were decorated with huge red stars on the turrets and on the hull. It was not always enough. In case of captured vehicles, blue-on-blue incidents were more numerous, especially when the Red Air Force was involved.

Hungarian tanks in the Red Army

The Soviet 18th Army established an independent tank battalion based on captured Hungarian materials on 09/09/1944. The 18th Army was able to capture a significant number of enemy tanks. The war booty was repaired on army level and re-enlisted under the red star.

Lt. Gen. Shuravljev, commander of the 18th Army ordered the technical chief of the Army to organise an independent tank battalion with 32 armoured vehicles.

The independent tank battalion numbered 40 officers, 138 NCOs and 28 enlisted men. The battalion consisted of three tank companies, plus the battalion staff and maintenance, support and the medical platoons. The tank companies consisted of three platoons. The battalion had one staff car, two motorbikes, 15 trucks, two tanker trucks and 32 tanks.

According to the order, the battalion was trained to operate on mountainous terrain. The battalion commander is unknown but the deputy was Capt. Koval.

The 1st company could evaluate and train for a month before going into action. They even performed an 800-kilometre-long driving test on difficult mountainous terrain. Due to proper training just a few technical breakdowns were registered during the march. The crew at the 2nd and 3rd companies was not so lucky. They arrived just three days before the operation and missed the conversation training. The actual war fighting was done by the 1st company in the area of Verecke – Ushgorod.

The battalion's baptism of fire happened on 15th September 1944. The tanks of the battalion were divided into teams of 3-4 tanks. These teams were subordinated to the infantry as mobile fire support. In some cases 5-7 tanks were deployed independently with infantry riding on the tanks as infantry support.

The tanks attacked twice without infantry support at the railway station of Osza. The battalion lost three tanks, two were knocked out, and one burned out. Finally the railway station was taken with the help of the infantry.

The battalion took the lead to capture Munkács on 26th October 1944.

At the end of October 1944 the battalion possessed 8 Turáns, 2 Toldi tanks, 3 Zrínyi assault howitzers and 2 Nimrod Sp AA/AT vehicles.

The remaining 13 armoured vehicles of the battalion were handed over to the 5th Guard Tank Brigade on 13th November. According to the order, the battalions had to assemble in the neighbouring areas. Three tanks and the logistic tail had to move to Nyizsnij Nyemecke. Four non operational tanks had to remain at Ushgorod. The remaining seven tanks (5 Turán, 2 Zrínyi) were in combat at Tarnovce on 14th November. On 20th November three Turán and one Toldi tanks operated in this area.

The 5th Guard Tank Brigade still had three Turán and one Toldi and Zrínyi each on 1st January 1945.

The Red Army did not only re-enlist and utilise the captured enemy equipment, it also evaluated it. Guard Col. Voronyinyim, the chief of the maintenance service of the 18th Army summarized his opinion on the captured Hungarian armoured vehicles on 11th November 1944.

According to his report, the Turán I, II tanks needed at least 15-20 minutes preheating before movement. The 75 and 40 mm guns were similarly mounted in the turret and were accurate. The machine guns were complicated but functioned well. The Turáns were easy to drive, but the control was complicated as well as the engine maintenance. The tank needed a relatively large radius to turn around.

The Toldi I, II tanks had smaller engines than the Turán tanks. The Toldi tanks were equipped with one 20 or 40 mm gun and one machine gun. The Toldis were fast, manoeuvrable and easy to drive.

The Zrínyi assault gun was equipped with one 105 mm howitzer. The Zrínyi was relatively small and manoeuvrable, which was an advantage in case of combat.

The Nimrod Sp AA/AT vehicles were armed with a gun with a 5-shell-magazine. It could be used against air and land targets. The Nimrod was best used as an infantry support vehicle. Its anti-tank capacity was limited.

The armoured vehicles listed above were best suited as infantry support. However, these tanks were inferior to the Soviet tanks. Due to their size, they were suitable to overcome narrow, difficult roads.

The evaluated armoured vehicles had very weak armoured protection. Every Soviet AT system could knock them out. The 37mm AT projectiles caused relatively light and easily repairable damage. Projectiles above 37 mm did significant or deadly harm on the Hungarian tanks. The rocket propelled or cumulative shells could easily burn out these vehicles.

ANNEX 2

Field Uniform, equipment of the armoured troops in WWII

The field uniforms of the armoured troops were basically identical to the uniforms of the army, but included some special protective and other clothes in accordance with the special needs of the armoured, motorised troops.

Protective clothing for armoured, motorcyclist troops

In the early years the secret armoured troops wore one or two-piece mechanic's overalls, several variants were used.

In 1936 armoured troops received their heavy two-piece brown leather 35M uniform. The leather tunic had strapped cuffs and brown crowned buttons and the trousers had strapped ankles. The tunic, by regulation, was worn tucked into the trousers to make movement inside the armoured vehicles easier. However, according to the photos it was mostly worn outside the trousers. The troops had the Italian style 37M leather crash helmet. The helmet was a deep-domed fibre crash helmet covered with black leather. A thick padded rim ran around the crown, and on the rear there was a leather neck-flap which extended backwards from the ears. The Italian helmet was designed without intercom equipment. The Hungarians developed their own version with earphones and brown leather cover and was designated as model 39M.

Under the leather 35M uniform the troops wore their field uniform, which was extremely hot in summer time. In spite of the short falls of the 35M uniform it was used until the end of the war.

On the other hand, a new two-piece German armoured uniform style was developed. It consisted of a smoke-gray short jacket and trousers and was worn with laced-up boots.

The assault artillery also used the 39M helmet. They were issued with one-piece canvas overalls with leather jerkins.

The motorcyclist troops used the 35M leather uniform with 37M crash helmets. The troops of the motorcycle-rifles companies were equipped with 35M steel helmets.

Bibliography

Published books in Hungarian (Author, title, name of the publisher, date of publication):

„Álltak Tordánál a csatát fejtőig vérben", Emlékkönyv a tordai csata 60. évfordulójára, 2004 Torda

Babucs Zoltán: Jászsági honvédek a II. világháborúban, I. A jászberényi harckocsi zászlóalj története a II. világháborúban, 2000

Babucs Zoltán – Maruzs Roland: „Jász vitézek rajta, előre!" A jászberényi kerékpáros és harckocsizó zászlóalj története 1920-1944, Puedlo

Balla Tibor – Csikány Tamás – Gulyás Géza – Horváth Csaba – Kovács Vilmos: A magyar tüzérség 100 éve, 1913-2013, Zrínyi 2014

Bangha Ernő: A magyar királyi testőrség 1920-1944, Európa 1990

Dr. Barczy Zoltán – Sárhidai Gyula : A Boforstól a Doráig, A magyar légvédelmi tüzérség 1914 – 1945, Petit Real, 2008

Bíró Ádám – Éder Miklós – Sárhidai Gyula: A magyar királyi honvédség külföldi gyártású páncélos harcjárművei 1920- 1945, Petit Real, 2006

Bíró Ádám – Éder Miklós – Sárhidai Gyula: A magyar királyi honvédség hazai gyártású páncélos harcjárművei 1920- 1945, Petit Real, 2012

Bombay László: A harckocsik története, Akadémia, 1990

Bombay László – Gyarmati József – Turcsányi Károly: Harckocsik 1916-tól napjainkig, Zrínyi

Bonhardt Attila – Sárhidai Gyula – Winkler : A magyar királyi honvédség fegyverzete 1919 45 1, Zrínyi, 1992

Dálnoki Veress Lajos: Magyarország honvédelme a II. világháború előtt és alatt (1920-1945), München, 1974

Dombrády Loránd-Tóth Lajos: Magyar Királyi Honvédség 1919-45, Zrínyi, 1987

Dombrády Loránd: A magyar gazdaság és a hadfelszerelés, 1938/44, Akadémia, 1981

Csima János: Források a Magyar Honvédség II. világháborús történetének tanulmányozásához, Zrínyi, 1961

Gosztonyi Péter. A Magyar Honvédség a II. világháborúban, Európa, 1992

Gögh Gábor – Monostori Péter: A magyar királyi testőrség képes krónikája 1920-1945, Militaria Hungarica, 2012

Görgey Vince: Páncélosok előre!, Stádium, 1942

György Sándor: A magyar királyi 16. honvéd felderítő osztály harcai az 1. hadsereg kötelékében 1944 – 1945, HistoriaAntik Kiadó 2012

BIBLIOGRAPHY

Hajdú Ferenc – Sárhidai Gyula: A magyar királyi honvéd Haditechnikai Intézettől a HM Technológiai Hivatalig, HM Technológiai Hivatal 2005

Horváth Csaba: A magyar katonai felderítés története a kezdetektől 1945-ig, Puedlo

Horváth Csaba – Lengyel Ferenc : A délvidéki hadművelet 1940, Puedlo

Illésfalvi Péter – Szabó Péter – Számvéber Norbert: Erdély a Hadak Útján 1940-1944, Puedlo

Illésfalvi Péter – Kovács Vilmos – Maruzs Roland: Vitézségért, HK Hermanos, 2011

Illésfalvi Péter: Erdélyi bevonulás, 1940, Tortoma 2010

Kaiser Ferenc: A magyar királyi csendőrség története a két világháború között, Pannónia Könyvek, 2002

Dr. Legány Dezső: Emlékei a doni harcokról, Turfi Kiadó, 2002

Dr. Lengyel: A 3. Magyar Királyi Hadsereg délvidéki hadműveletei, ZMNK

Maertens György: A RÁBA Gyár története, KÖZDOK, 1980

Magyarország a II. világháborúban, Enciklopédia, PETIT REAL, 1997

Mányi Pál: Magyar páncélosokkal a hadak útján 1941-1944, 2000

Számvéber Norbert: Az alföldi páncélos csata, Puedlo

Számvéber Norbert: Páncélos hadviselés a budapesti csatában, Puedlo

Számvéber Norbert: Páncélosok a Felvidéken, Puedlo

Szabó Péter: Don-kanyar, Zrínyi, 1994

Szabó Péter: Don-kanyar, Corvina 2001

Szabó Péter – Számvéber Norbert: A keleti hadszíntér és Magyarország 1941- 1943, Puedlo

Szabó Péter – Számvéber Norbert: Magyarország és a keleti hadszíntér 1943-1945, Puedlo

Rada Tibor: A magyar királyi honvéd Ludovika Akadémia és testvérintézetek összefoglaló története 1930-1945, GÁLOS NYOMDÁSZ Bt, 1998

Ravasz István : Erdély, mint hadszíntér 1944, PETIT REAL, 1997

Stark: Hadak Útján, Corvina, 1991

Sőregi Zoltán – Végső István: Gyorsan, bátran, hűséggel, A m. kir. „Balogh Ádám" 15. honvéd kerékpáros zászlóalj története, Timp Kiadó 2009

Sőregi Zoltán: Katonák kerékpáron, A magyar királyi honvédség kerékpáros tisztjeinek adattára 1920-1945, Magánkiadás 2014

Dr. Tóth László: A magyar királyi honvédség egyenruhái 1926-1945, HUNIFORM, 2009

Turcsányi Károly: Nehéz harckocsik, Puedlo

Ungváry Krisztián: Budapest ostroma, Corvina, 1998

Ungváry Krisztián: A magyar honvédség a második világháborúban, Osiris, 2005

Dr. Vajda Ferenc: A Don partjáig és vissza, Puedlo

Dr. Varga D. József: Magyar autógyárak katonai járművei
Maróti, 2008

Dr. Varga D. József: Magyar harc- és gépjárműfejlesztések története
MH kiadvány

Veress D. Csaba: A Dunántúl hadi krónikája 1944/45, Zrínyi, 1984

Veress D. Csaba: Balatoni Csata 1944/45, Veszprém Megyei kiadványok, 1977

Veress D. Csaba: Magyarország hadikrónikája 1944-1945 I.-II. Militaria 2002

Zachár Sándor: Katonai Zseb-lexikon, 1939

Articles:
ZMKA Akadémiai Közlemények:
Horváth Csaba: A Gyorshadtest felderítő szolgálata a
Jugoszlávia elleni háborúban, 1991/182

Jakus János: A magyar királyi 3. hadsereg megalakulása és hadműveletei (1944. szeptember-október), 1994/204

Dr. Lengyel Ferencz: M. kir. I. Gyors Hadtest hadműveletei a Szu elleni háborúban 1941 július 9. november 15., 1994/204

Makláry László. Egy kis háborús magántörténelem, 1993/193

Hadtörténeti Közlemények:
Tóth Lajos: A Gyorshadtest a Szovjetunióban, HK 1966/2

Dombrándy Loránd: A horthysta katonai vezetés erőfeszítései a páncélos fegyvernem megteremtésére, HK 1969/2, 1970/4

Jakus János: A Magyar 3. Hadsereg harcai 1944. szeptember 22- november 3. között, HK 1995/1

Jakus János: A m. kir. IV. hadtest támadó hadműveletei 1944 szeptemberében, HK 1994/1

Haditechnikai Szemle:
Bíró Ádám: A 40/43M Zrínyi rohamtarack kifejlesztése és használata, 3. rész, 1996/4

Bíró Ádám: T-38 harckocsi a Magyar királyi Honvédség használatában, 1993/4

Bíró Ádám: A 44M Tass nehéz harckocsi tervei 1943/44, 1993/1

Bíró Ádám: A magyar páncélos fegyvernem kezdetei, az LK-II és FIAT-3000B harckocsik, 1993/2

Bíró Ádám: The AC-II, 39M Csaba páncélgépkocsik, 1992/3

Bíró Ádám: A magyar páncélos fegyvernem kezdetei, 2. rész, a FIAT Ansaldo 35M, 1993/3

Bíró Ádám: a Turán II és Turán III harckocsi család, 1. rész, 1995/3

Bíró Ádám: A 40M Turán típusú harckocsi megalkotása, 3. rész, 1995/2

Bíró Ádám: A 40M Turán harckocsi megalkotása, 2. rész, 1995/1

Bíró Ádám: A Turán II es a Turán III harckocsi család, 2. rész, 1995/4

Bíró Ádám: A 40/43M Zrínyi rohamtarack kifejlesztése és alkalmazása, 2. rész, 1996/2

Bíró Ádám: A 40/43M Zrínyi rohamtarack kifejlesztése és alkalmazása, l. rész, 1996/1

Bíró Ádám: A 40M Turán harckocsi kifejlesztése 1. rész, 1994/4

Bíró Ádám: A 40M Nimród páncélvadász- önjáró légvédelmi gépágyú, 1. rész, 1994/2

Bíró Ádám: A 40M Nimród páncélvadász- önjáró légvédelmi gépágyú, 2.rész, 1994/3

Bíró Ádám: Az első magyar tervezésű harckocsi a V-4, 1992/4

Bíró Ádám: Magyar, Marder páncélvadász Toldi alvázon, 1990/4

Bonhardt Attila: Pz.Kpfw. VI E Tiger harckocsik a Magyar

Katona Újság:
Számvéber Norbert: Nimród páncélgépágyú Urivnál, 2010/1.

Számvéber Norbert: A magyar 1. önálló páncélvadász század rövid története, 1943, 2010/3.

Sőregi Zoltán: Adalékok a galántai csendőr karhatalmi zászlóalj történetéhez, 2011/1.

Szabó Kristóf: A 101. önálló harckocsi század vázlatos története, 2011/5.

Simon Tamás: Az 1. gépkocsizó dandár a nyikolajevi csatában, 2013/4.

Militaria Modell:
Barcy Zoltán: 40M Nimród, 1992/4

Bíró Ádám: 44M Tass nehézharckocsi, 1992/5

Bonhardt Attila: Kísérleti magyar páncélvadász, 1992/2

Éder Miklós: Magyar páncélos járművek alakulat jelzései, 1. rész, 1991/1

Éder Miklós: Magyar páncélos járművek alakulat jelzései, 2. rész, 1991/2

Éder Miklós: 38M Toldi könnyű harckocsi, 1991/3

Éder Miklós: 39M Csaba páncélgépkocsi, 1992/1

Éder Miklós: LK-II harckocsi a Magyar Honvédségnél, 1992/2

Éder Miklós: Magyar páncélos csapatok bőrruházata, 1992/4

Éder Miklós: Magyar páncélosok hadi jelzése, 1917-1945, 1992/6

Pro Modell
Mujzer Péter: A magyar királyi honvédség páncélos csapatainak jelzésrendszere, 2003/1-3

András Palásthy: Bapteme du feu mortel en Ukraine, Batailles&Blindes n.42

Steel Masters n.8, Les blindes de l'Axe, 2010

Unpublished materials:
Móker: Hadinapló a 30/II harckocsi zászlóalj 1942.-es Doni harcairól

HARCTUDÓSÍTÁS, A 2. páncéloshadosztály Nadvorna- Tlumaczky-Sloboda Lesna-i harcai 1944. április 13. – május 14.

HL I. 89. VKF 306 doboz, VKF 634/hdm.csf.-1944.

Foreign Books:

David Ansell: Military Motorcycles, Osprey, 1996

Max Axworthy: Third Axis Fourth Ally, Arms and Armour, 1995

Dr Tamás Baczoni – Dr László Tóth: Hungarian Army Uniforms 1939 – 1945, HUNIFORM 2010

Csaba Becze: Magyar steel, Mashroom Publication, 2006

Boj u Ozera Balaton janvar-Mart 1945, Tankovije Srazhenija 1998

Ruppert Butler: Hitler's Jackals, Leo Cooper, 1998

Patrick Cloutier: Three Kings: Axis Royal Armies on the Russian Front 1941, 2014

Terry J. Gander: The 40mm Bofors Gun, 1986 Patrick Stephens Ltd.

Peter Gosztonyi: Deutschlands waffengefahrten an de rost front 1941-1941, Motorbuch Verlag, 1981

George Forty: World War Two AFVs, Osprey, 1998

George Forty: World War Two Tanks, Osprey, 1996

George Forty: Word War Two Tanks, Osprey, 1995

Jeffry Fowler: Axis Cavalry in World War II, Osprey, 2001

Werner Haupt: Army Group South, Schiffer, 1998

Charles Kliment- Vladimir Francev: Czechoslovakian AFVs 1918-1948, Schiffer, 1997

Charles Kliment – Bretislav Nakláda: Germany's First Ally, Schiffer 1997

Maksim Kolomiets – Ilia Mosanskij: Trofei v Krasnoj Armij 1941-1945, Frontovaja Illustracija 1999

Janusz Ledwoch: Eastern Front 1941-45, Militaria, 1995

Victor Madej: South-Eastern Europe Axis Armies Handbook, Game Marketing Company, 1982

Military Intelligence Division: Order of Battle and Handbook of the Hungarian Armed Forces, 1944 US War Dep. (restricted)

Janusz Magnuski: Armour in Profile 1, PELTA, 1997

Perry Moore: Panzerschlacht, Armored operations ont he Hungarian plains September-November, Helion, 2008

Péter Mujzer: Hungarian Mobile Forces 1920-45, Bayside Books, 2000

Péter Mujzer: Huns on Wheels, Hungarian Mobile Forces 1920-1945

Leo Niehorster: The Royal Hungarian Army 1920-45, Bayside Books, 1998

Janusz Pielkalkiewicz: The Cavalry 1939-45, Macdonald, 1986

Janusz Pielkalkiewicz: Tank War 1939-1945, Guild Publishing, 1986

Jean Restayn: Tiger I on the Eastern Front, Histoire&Collection

Jean Restayn: WWII tank encyclopedia in color 1939-1945, Histoire&Collection

Ronald Tarnstrom: Balkan Battles, Trogen Books, 1998

Nigel Thomas- László Pál Szabó: The Royal Hungarian Army in World War II, Ospery, 2008

Rex Trye: Mussolini's Soldiers, Motorbooks International, 1995

Anthony Tucker-Jones: Armored warfare and Hitler's allies 1941-1945, Pen&Sword, 2013

Anthony Tucker-Jones: Armored warfare ont he Eastern Front, Pen&Sword, 2011

Anthony Tucker-Jones: The battle for Budapest1944-1945, Pen&Sword, 2016

Jonathan Trigg: Death on the Don, Spellmount, 2013

Steven Zaloga: Armored trains, Osprey, 2008

Steven Zaloga- James Grandsen: The Eastern Front, Arms and Armour, 1983

Steven Zaloga: Tanks of Hitler's eastern allies 1941-45, Osprey, 2013

Ian Walker: Iron hulls, iron hearts, Mussolini's elitte armoured divisiomm

Charles Winchester: Ostfront, Hitlers war on Russia 1941-1945, Osprey, 1998

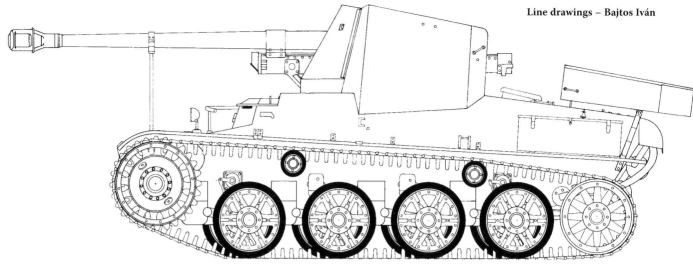

Line drawings – Bajtos Iván

Toldi tank hunter on the chassis of the 38. M Toldi light tank armed with 7,5cm anti-tank gun

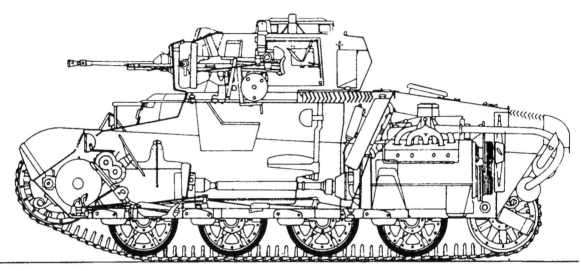

38. M Toldi I light tank sectional view

37. M 40mm tank gun used in V-4 and Toldi II experimental vehicles

Front view of the skirt plated 38. M Toldi II light tank

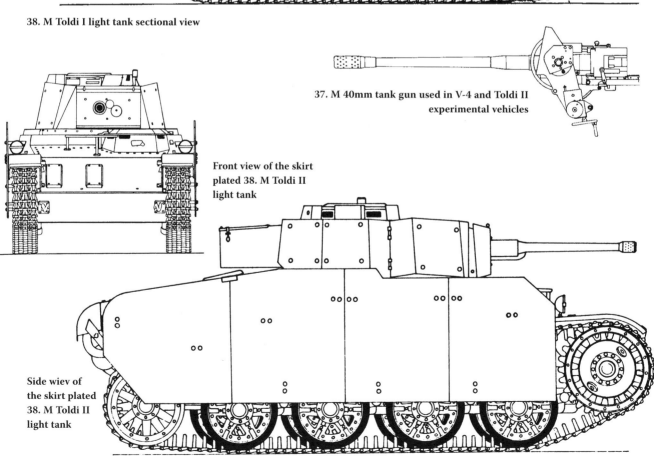

Side wiev of the skirt plated 38. M Toldi II light tank

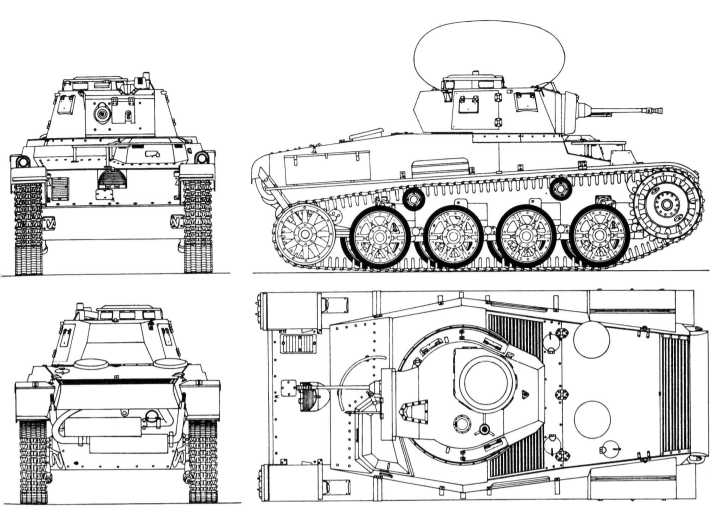

Four view of the 38. M Toldi I light tank

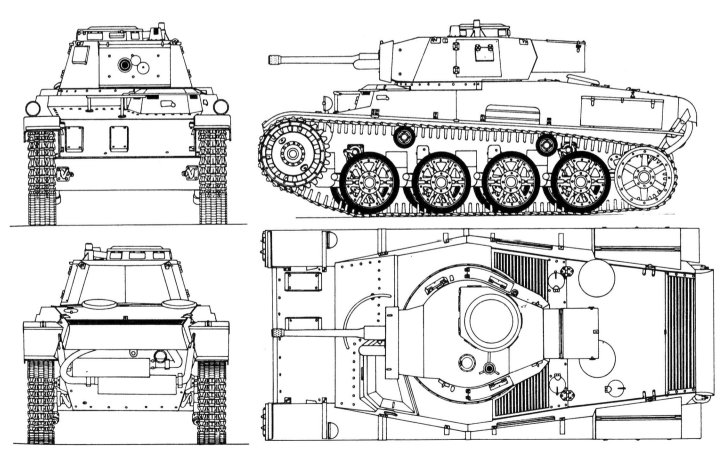

Four view of the 38. M Toldi IIA light tank

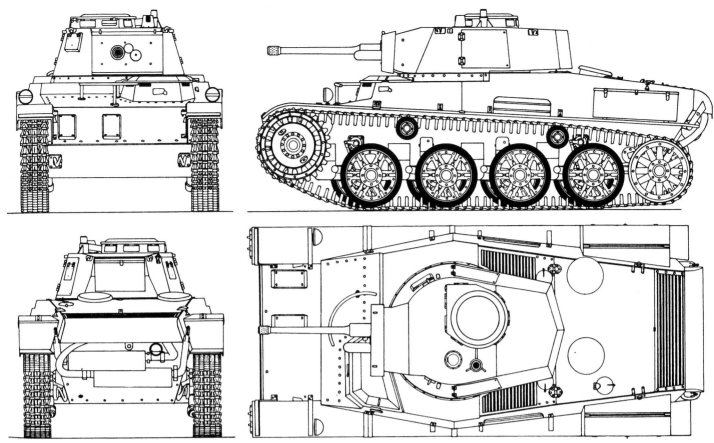

Four view of the 38. M Toldi III light tank

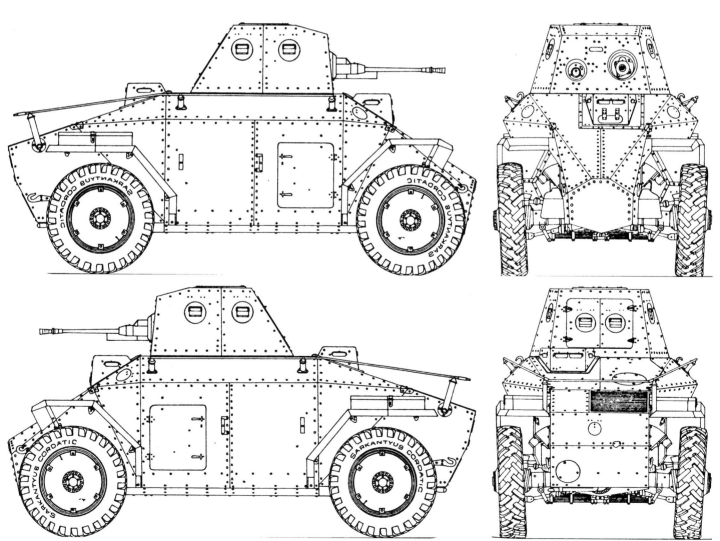

Four view of the 39. M Csaba armoured car

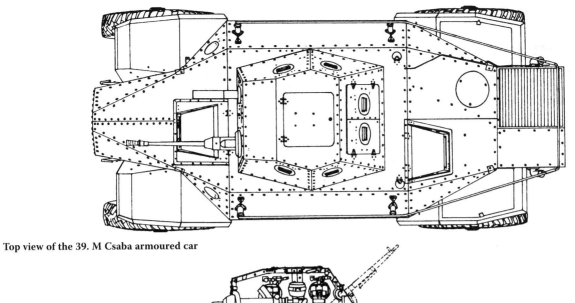

Top view of the 39. M Csaba armoured car

Sectional view of the 39. M Csaba armoured car

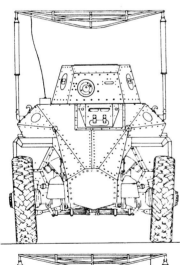
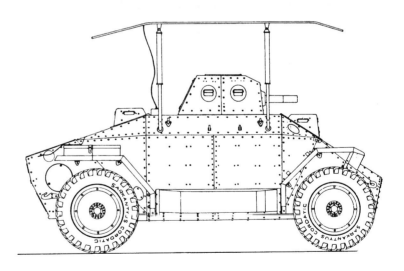

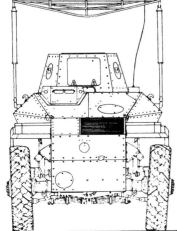
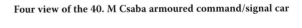

Four view of the 40. M Csaba armoured command/signal car

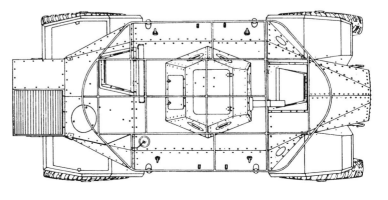

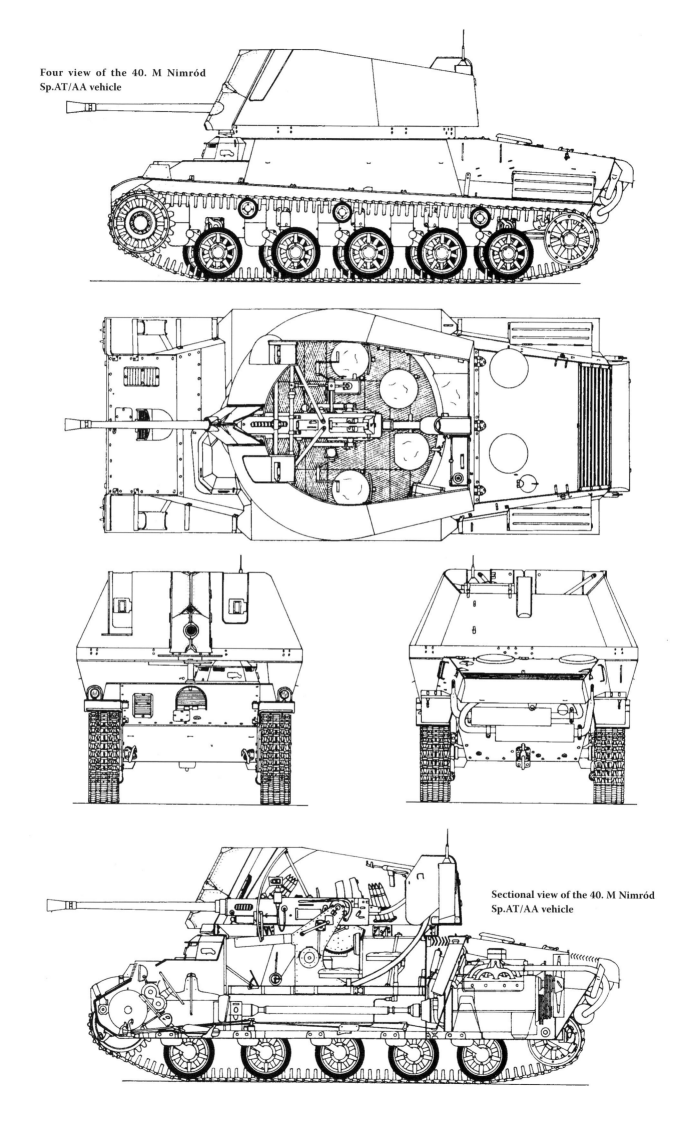

Four view of the 40. M Nimród
Sp.AT/AA vehicle

Sectional view of the 40. M Nimród
Sp.AT/AA vehicle

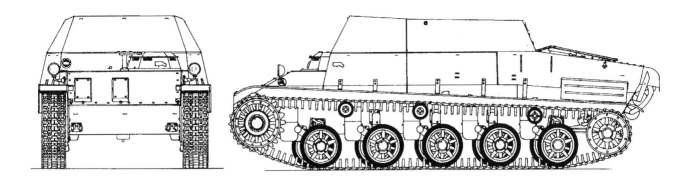

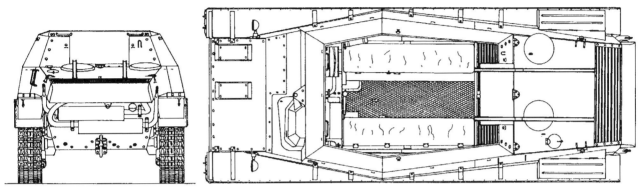

Four view of the 43. M Lehel armoured vehicle

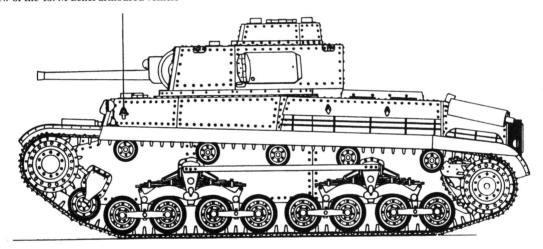

Side view of the 40. M Turán medium tank

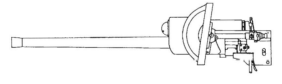

41. M 40mm tank gun used in 40. M
Turán medium tank

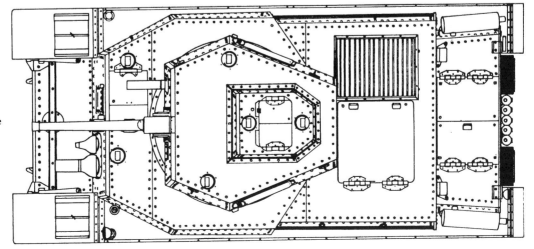

Top view of the
40. M Turán
medium tank

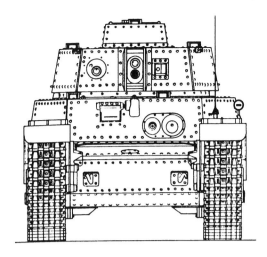
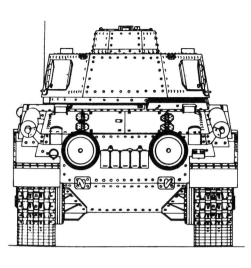

Front and rear view
of the 40. M Turán
medium tank

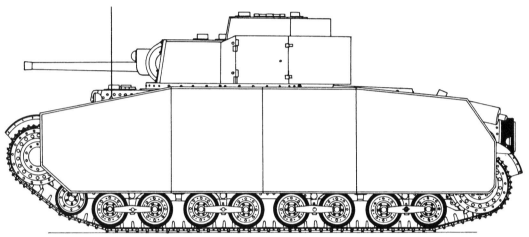

Side view of the skirt plated 40. M Turán medium tank

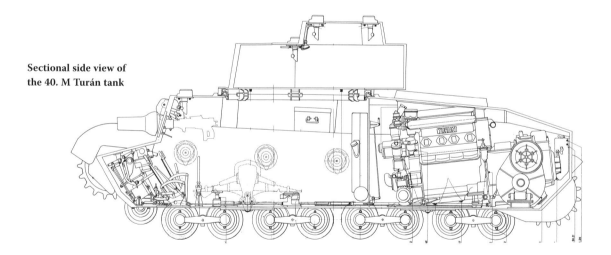

Sectional side view of
the 40. M Turán tank

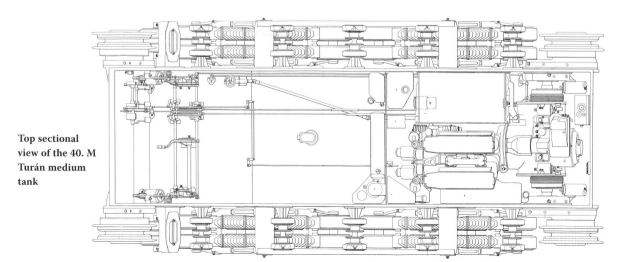

Top sectional
view of the 40. M
Turán medium
tank

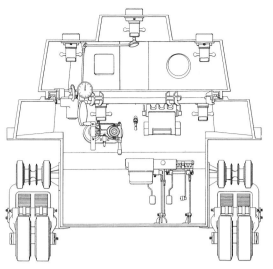

Frontal sectional view of the 40. M Turán tank

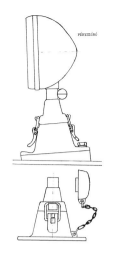

Headlight of the Turán tanks

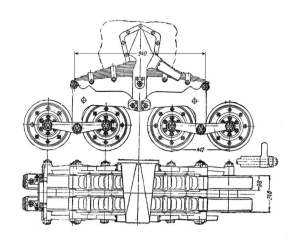

Elliptic sprung with wheel bogie of the Turán tanks

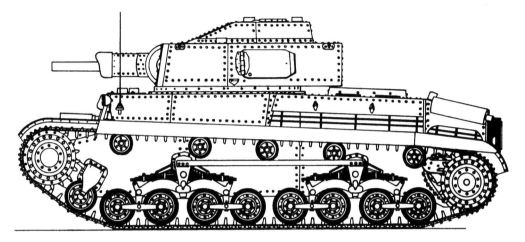

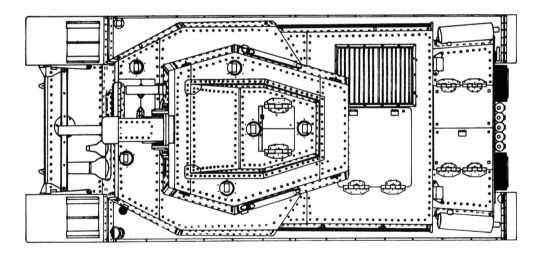

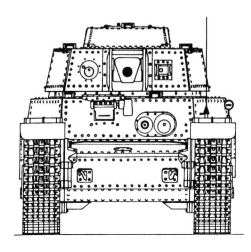

Four view of the 41. M Turán heavy tank

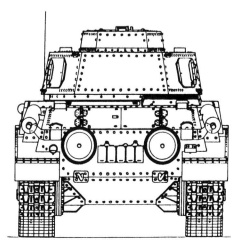

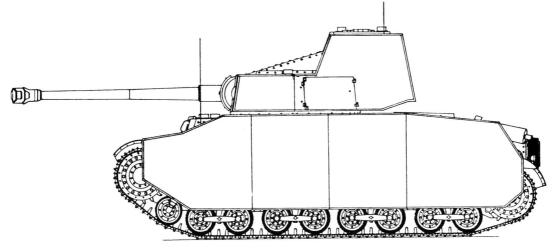

Side view of the skirt plated 43. M Turán III heavy tank

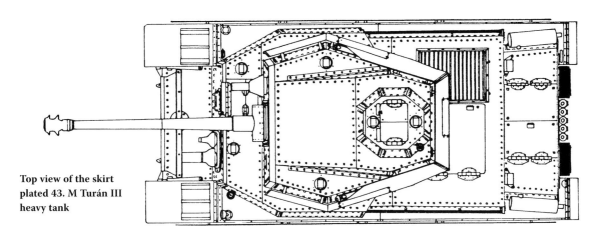

Top view of the skirt plated 43. M Turán III heavy tank

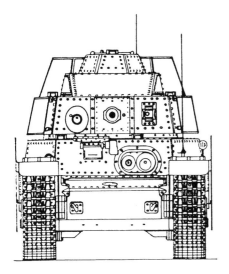

Front and rear view of the skirt plated 43. M Turán III heavy tank

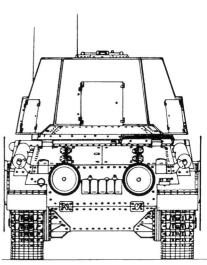

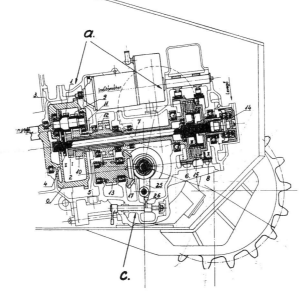

Sectional view of the gear box of the Turán tanks

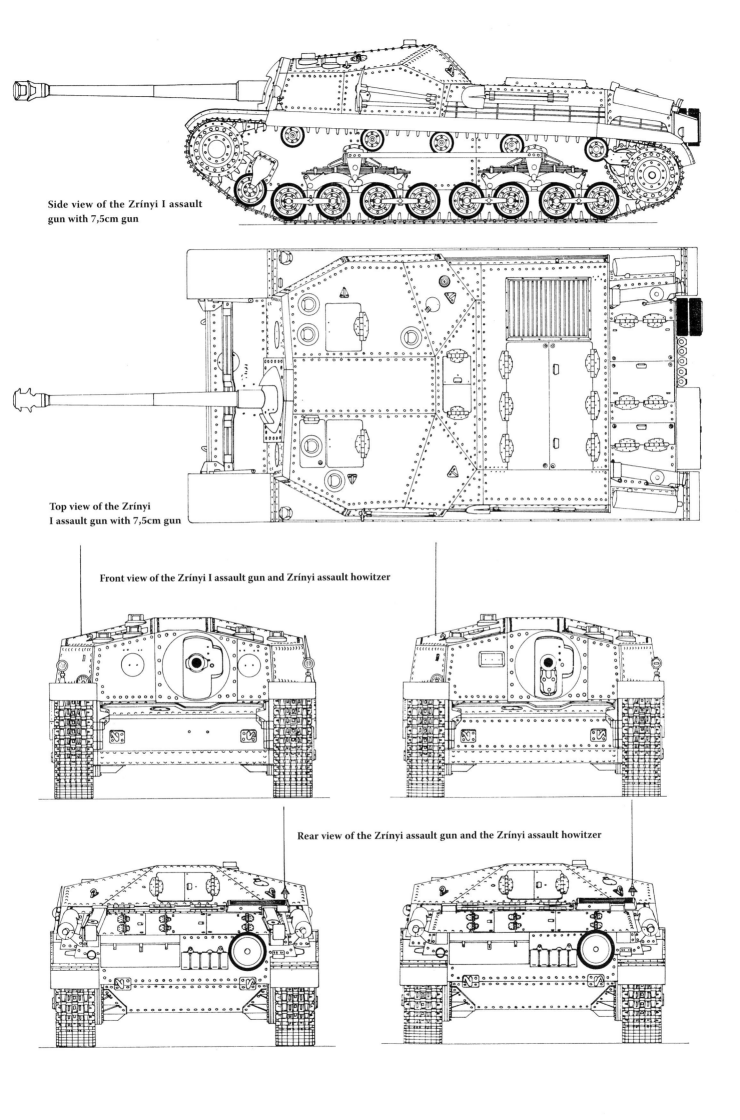

Side view of the Zrínyi I assault gun with 7,5cm gun

Top view of the Zrínyi I assault gun with 7,5cm gun

Front view of the Zrínyi I assault gun and Zrínyi assault howitzer

Rear view of the Zrínyi assault gun and the Zrínyi assault howitzer

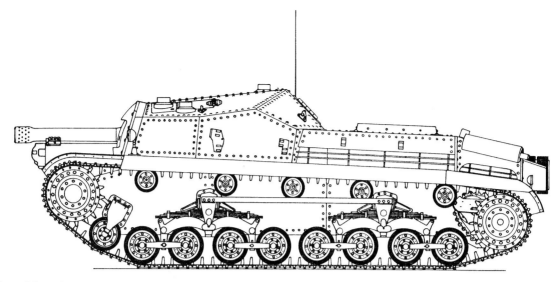

Side view of the 40/43. M Zrínyi assault howitzer

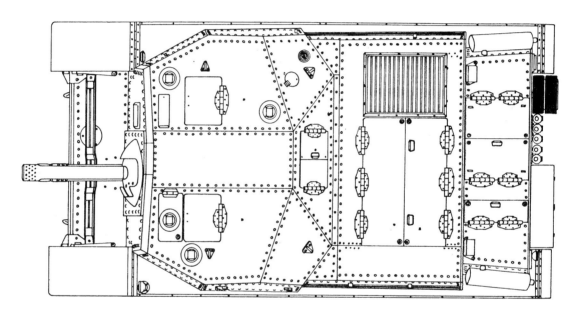

Top view of the 40/43. M Zrínyi assault howitzer

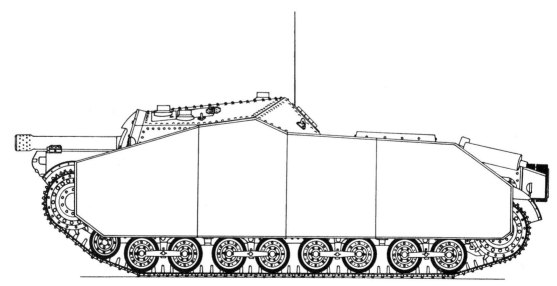

Side view of the skirt plated 40/43. M Zrínyi assault howitzer

40. M Turán medium tank painted in three tones camouflage and late style military insignia at the yards of the Automobile Depot of the Army at Mátyásföld, 1943. [coloured by Deák Tamás]

38. M Toldi light tank painted in three tones camouflage and octagonal military insignia exhibited on a military display for the civilians. [coloured by Deák Tamás

FIAT-Pavesi P4-100 artillery tractor painted in dark olive green, with protective canvas cover, the main artillery tractor of the army in the 30s. [coloured by Tamás Deák]

Factory fresh 41. M Turán heavy tanks at the Automobile Depot of the Army, the tanks painted in three tones camouflage, the military and unit signs not yet painted. [coloured by Deák Tamás]

Short lunch break of the officers of a horse drawn supply column, during the occupation of Transylvania in September 1940. [original colour photo from Fortepan]

The prototype of the 41. M Turán signal tank painted in three tone camouflage with late style military insignia, armed with dummy gun. [coloured by Deák Tamás]

40. M Turán medium tanks on trial before taken over by the Army Acceptance Committee, the tanks operated by civilian, factory crew. Painted in dark olive green camouflage. [coloured by Deák Tamás]

Advancing troops of 3. Tank Regiment at Nadworna, April 1944, Galicia. The 40. M Turán medium tank leading the Skoda and Mercedes staff cars followed by a despatch rider. [coloured by Deák Tamás]

Advancing Hungarian and German tanks at Nadworna, April 1944. In front of the 40. M Turán tank a German Pz. IV.H tank still wearing the winter camouflage. The tactical number of the Turán was overpainted by the censor. [coloured by Deák Tamás]

Hungarian Pz.IV.F2 tank wears the origional German grey camouflage, handed over by the German to replace the losses at the 1. Armoured Field Division in 1942, River Don. [coloured by Deák Tamás]

Hungarian reconnaissance team in Ukraine, summer of 1941, armed with 31. M light machinegun and 39. M Csaba armoured car. [coloured by Deák Tamás]

Skoda 38(t) tanks served at the 1. Armoured field Division, the tactical number on the turret, 30/I Tank Battalion, 2. Company, battalion staff. The Skoda tanks arrived in German grey colour, the octagonal military insignia not yet painted. [coloured by Deák Tamás]

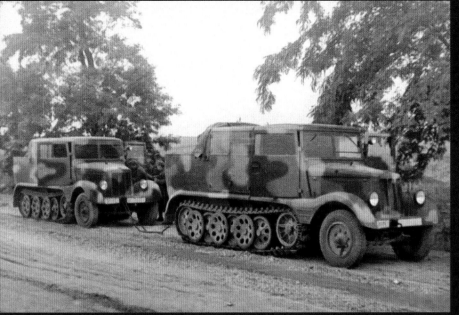

37. M Hansa Lloyd half-tracked artillery tractors produced with Hungarian body, for towing the Bofors guns and light field howitzers at the Mobile Corps. These Hansa Lloyd tractors painted in three tones camouflage. [coloured by Deák Tamás]

Armoured car company equipped with 39. M Csaba armoured cars and a G5 Mercedes staff car, the vehicles painted in three tone camouflage. [coloured by Deák Tamás]

Ford truck belonged to the supply column negotiate a difficult mountainous terrain in 1941 Carpathian Mountains, the truck painted in three tone camouflage, except the canvas canopy. [coloured by Deák Tamás]

39. M Csaba armoured car painted in factory fresh dark olive green camouflage, and small size military insignia. [coloured by Deák Tamás]

40. M Turán medium tanks on official trial before taken over by the Army Acceptance Committee, the tanks operated by civilian, factory crew. Painted in dark olive green camouflage. [coloured by Deák Tamás]

38. M Toldi tanks at the Automobile Depot, painted in dark olive green camouflage, with late style military insignia and Mechanised Branch sign. [coloured by Deák Tamás]

38. M Botond truck wears the three tone camouflage, canvas canopy also in a same colour. [coloured by Pálinkás Zsolt]

Painted by Arkadiusz Wróbel

38. M Toldi light tank belonged to the 1. Light Tank Company of the 1. Armoured Cavalry Battalion, September 1940, occupation of Transylvania, white Turul bird with sword was the unit insignia of the light tank company.

38. M Toldi light tank belonged to the 9. Bicycle-Tank Battalion wears the standard octagonal military insignia and next to it the Mechanised Branch insignia on the turret, summer of 1941 Ukraine.

Painted by Arkadiusz Wróbel

38. M Toldi light tank up gunned with 40mm gun, the light tank belonged to the 2. Armoured Division and was captured by Soviet forces in summer of 1944, Galicia. The Toldi light tank has the late war military insignia and three tone camouflage.

38. M Toldi belonged to the 1. Cavalry Tank Battalion, have the standard olive green camouflage with late style military insignia an Mechanised Branch sign on the turret, in Poland summer of 1944.

Painted by Arkadiusz Wróbel

39. M Csaba armoured car have the standard olive green camouflage with late style military insignia, probably belonged to the armoured car company of one of the reconnaissance battalion.

39. M Csaba armoured car belonged to the 1. Reconnaissance Battalion with Maltese cross military insignia and three tone camouflage, September 1940, occupation of Transylvania.

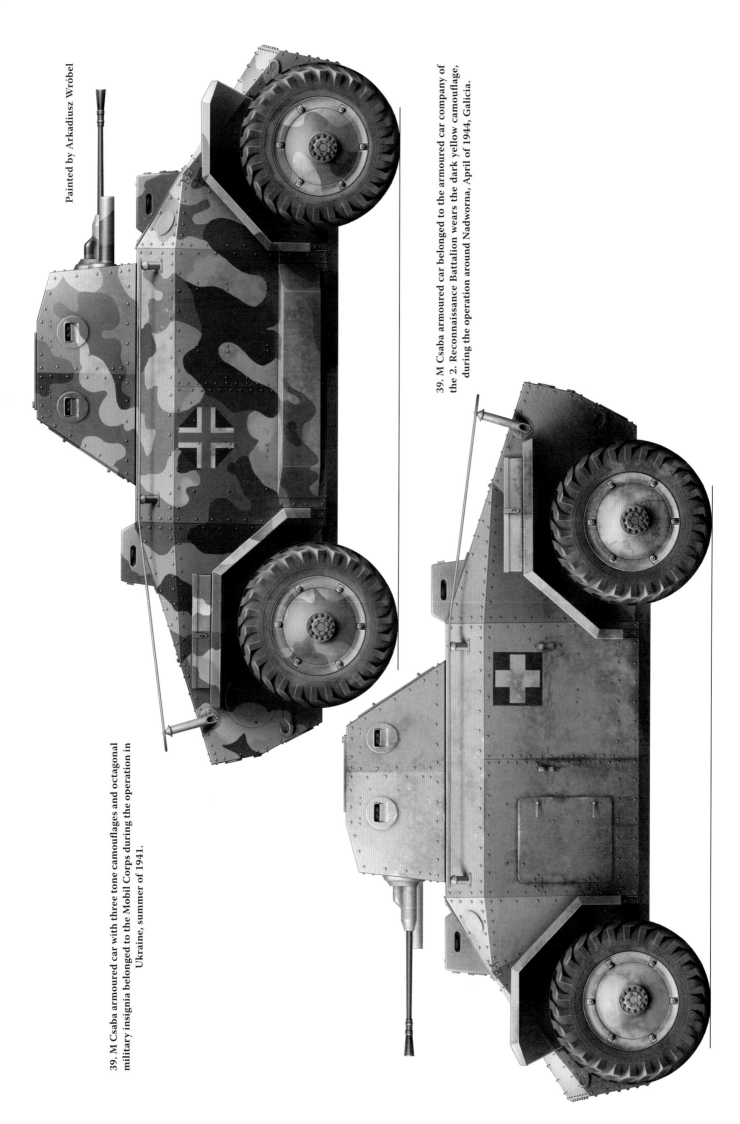

Painted by Arkadiusz Wróbel

39. M Csaba armoured car with with three tone camouflages and octagonal military insignia belonged to the Mobil Corps during the operation in Ukraine, summer of 1941.

39. M Csaba armoured car belonged to the armoured car company of the 2. Reconnaissance Battalion wears the dark yellow camouflage, during the operation around Nadworna, April of 1944, Galicia.

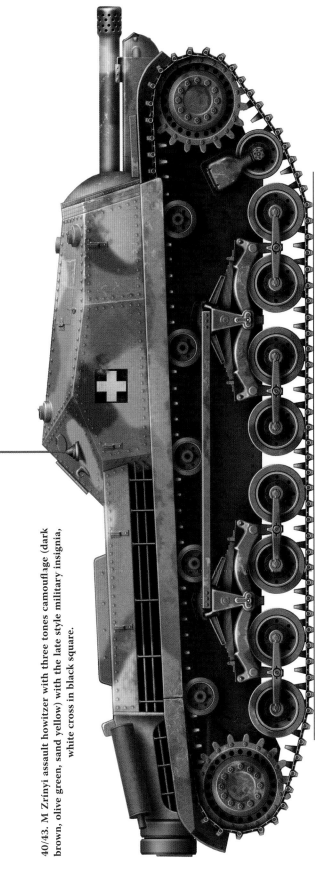

Painted by Arkadiusz Wróbel

The prototype of the 40/43. M Zrínyi assault howitzer with three tone camouflage at Hajmáskér artillery training field, evaluation course in 1943, without military insignia.

40/43. M Zrínyi assault howitzer with three tones camouflage (dark brown, olive green, sand yellow) with the late style military insignia, white cross in black square.

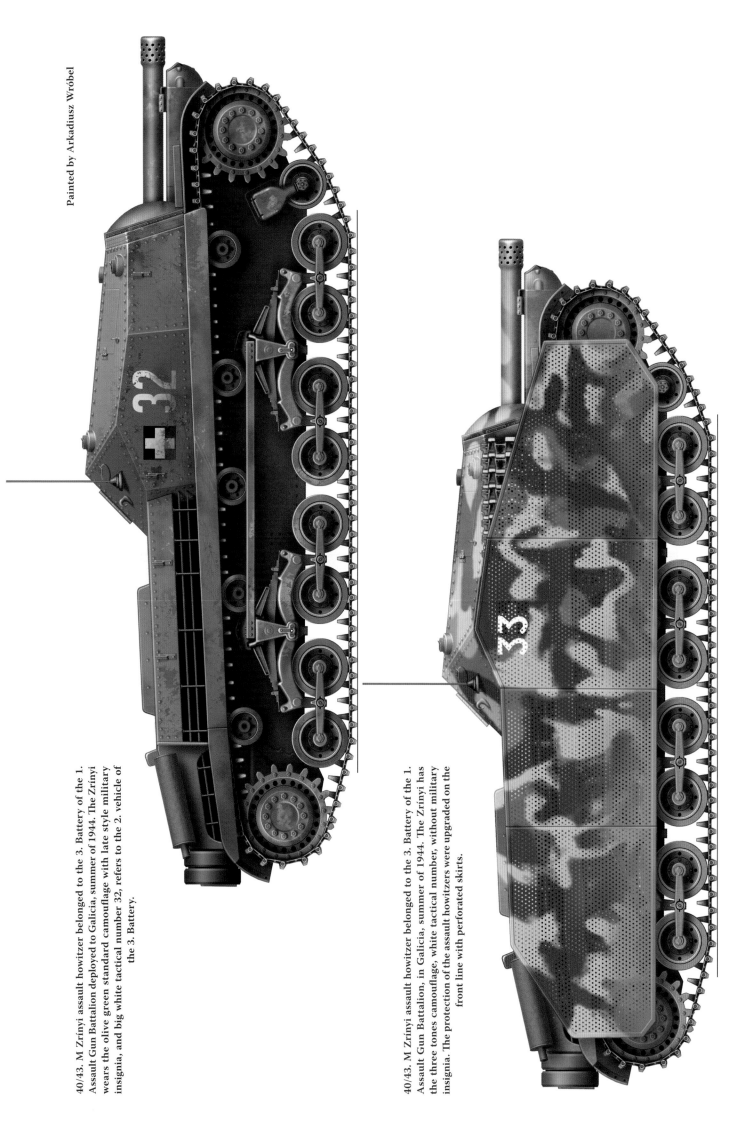

Painted by Arkadiusz Wróbel

40/43. M Zrínyi assault howitzer belonged to the 3. Battery of the 1. Assault Gun Battalion deployed to Galicia, summer of 1944. The Zrínyi wears the olive green standard camouflage with late style military insignia, and big white tactical number 32, refers to the 2. vehicle of the 3. Battery.

40/43. M Zrínyi assault howitzer belonged to the 3. Battery of the 1. Assault Gun Battalion, in Galicia, summer of 1944. The Zrínyi has the three tones camouflage, white tactical number, without military insignia. The protection of the assault howitzers were upgraded on the front line with perforated skirts.

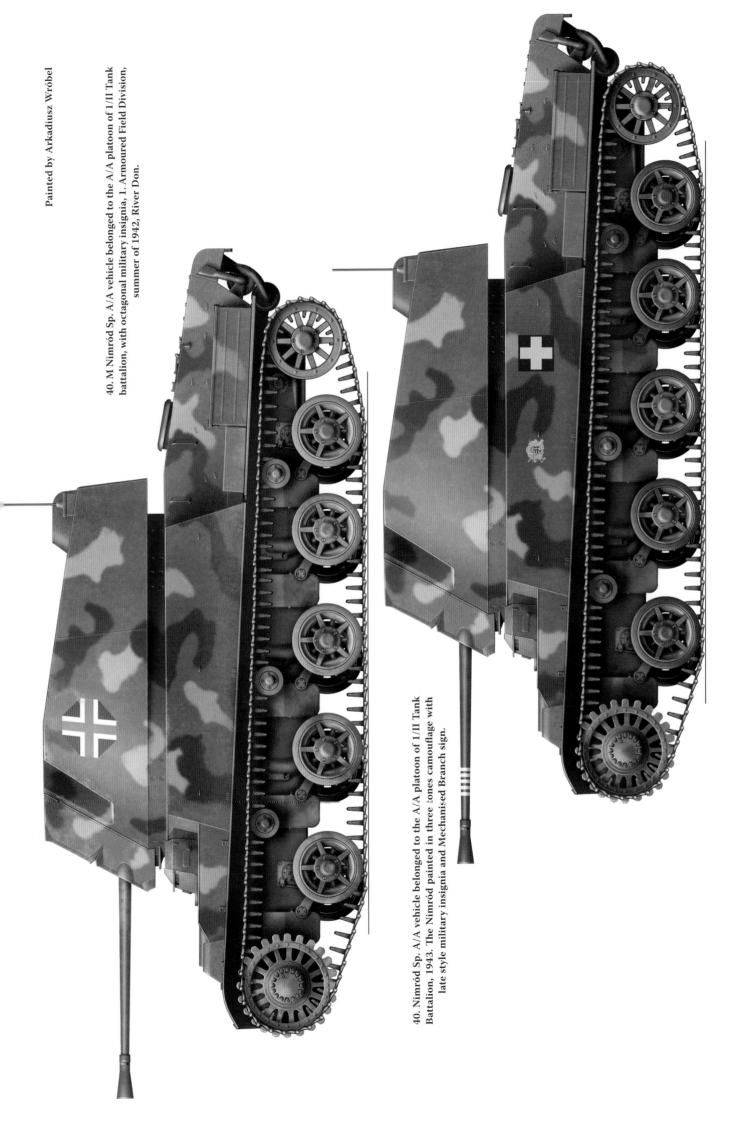

Painted by Arkadiusz Wróbel

40. M Nimród Sp. A/A vehicle belonged to the A/A platoon of 1/II Tank battalion, with octagonal military insignia, 1. Armoured Field Division, summer of 1942, River Don.

40. Nimród Sp. A/A vehicle belonged to the A/A platoon of 1/II Tank Battalion, 1943. The Nimród painted in three tones camouflage with late style military insignia and Mechanised Branch sign.

40. Nimród Sp. A/A vehicle, with standard dark olive green camouflage, late style military insignia and Mechanised Branch sign, 1944.

40. Nimród Sp. A/A vehicle, with winter camouflage, late style military insignia, winter of 1944-1945.

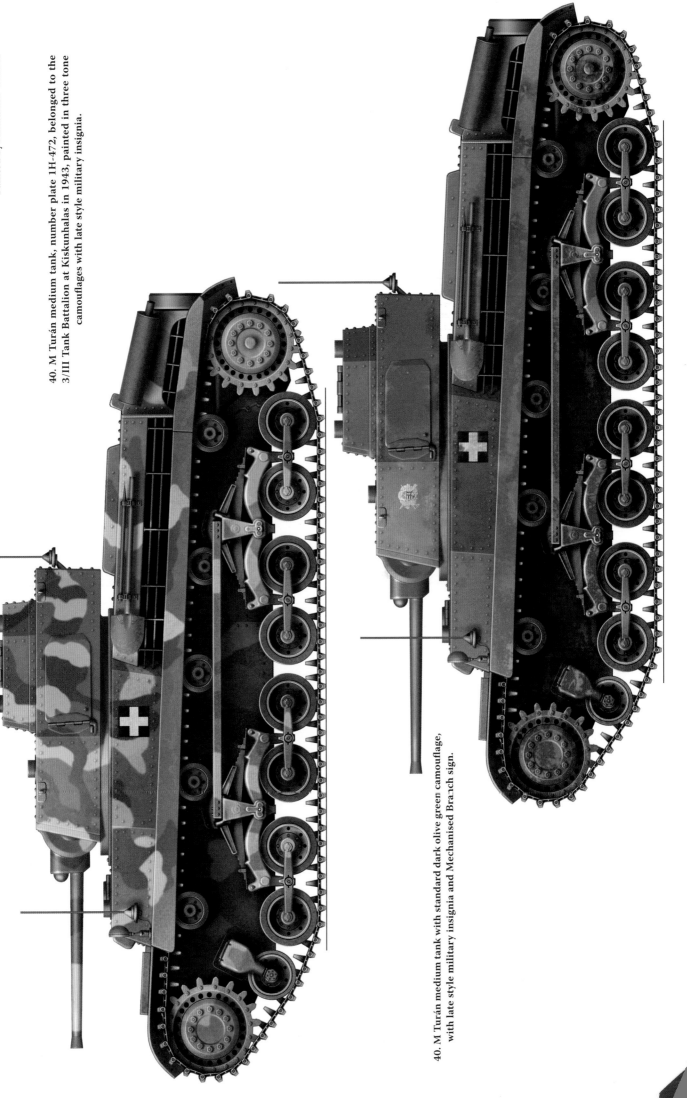

Painted by Arkadiusz Wróbel

40. M Turán medium tank, number plate 1H-472, belonged to the 3/III Tank Battalion at Kiskunhalas in 1943, painted in three tone camouflages with late style military insignia.

40. M Turán medium tank with standard dark olive green camouflage, with late style military insignia and Mechanised Branch sign.

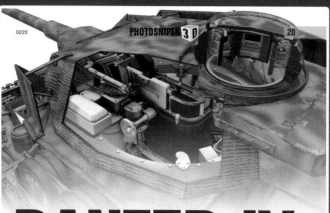